101 MAGIC TRICKS

ANY TIME, ANY PLACE

BRYAN MILES

QUARRY

Quarto is the authority on a wide range of topics.

Quarto educates, entertains and enriches the lives of our readers—enthusiasts and lovers of hands-on living.

www.QuartoKnows.com

© 2016 Quarto Publishing Group USA Inc.
Text © 2016 Aidan Knott
Photography © 2016 Sam Burrows

First published in the United States of America in 2016 by Quarry Books, an imprint of Quarto Publishing Group USA Inc.
100 Cummings Center
Suite 406-L
Beverly, Massachusetts 01915-6101
Telephone: (978) 282-9590
Fax: (978) 283-2742
QuartoKnows.com
Visit our blogs at QuartoKnows.com

10 9 8 7 6 5 4 3 2 1

ISBN: 978-1-63159-072-6

Digital edition published in 2016
eISBN: 978-1-62788-843-1

Library of Congress Cataloging-in-Publication Data
Miles, Bryan.
101 magic tricks: discover powerful magic for every occasion / Bryan Miles.
pages cm
Includes index.
ISBN 978-1-63159-072-6
1. Magic tricks. I. Title. II. Title: One hundred one magic tricks. III. Title: One hundred and one magic tricks.
GV1547.M52 2015
793.8--dc23
2015025881

Design: Burge Agency
Photography: Sam Burrows

Printed in China

CONTENTS

**FOR MOM, DAD, AND DYLAN—
FOR BEING THE REAL MAGIC IN MY LIFE
AND FOR ALWAYS BELIEVING IN ME.**

THE ART OF MAGIC IS AMAZING IN SO MANY WAYS!

TO EXPERIENCE MAGIC IS ASTONISHING . . . TO EXPERIENCE ENTERTAINING OTHERS WITH MAGIC IS EXHILARATING.

I have been involved in training young magicians and entertainers for thirty-five years, and what I have found remarkable is the "magic" it brings into the lives of those who set about learning and performing it. From the delight of discovering a new secret, through playing with how to transform it into an illusion, to sharing that illusion with a friend, colleague, or even a large audience, there are many dimensions of excitement awaiting you.

The benefits of learning magic are now well known—improved self-confidence, public speaking ability, organizational proficiency, and many other life skills. Perhaps the most significant gain of learning magic is that of stimulating your creativity. Magicians are known to be resourceful individuals, and this is no coincidence. Playing with, thinking about, and imagining magical illusions arouse the creative process. In an age in which information is so freely available, the ability to be innovative around information has become vital.

You have in your hands an exceptional opportunity to start learning, or if you already do magic, to take your interest further. Bryan Miles has opened the world of magic in a special way by giving fresh takes on old classics and creating new miracles while carefully taking the reader by the hand through the expansive area of presentation. Miles also introduces his special brand of magic in various areas of daily living, providing useful real-life situation clues to making your magic powerful. The layout of the book allows you to easily adapt the magic effects according to your style and to enter the world of magic in your chosen way.

Bryan Miles has a professional background in both education and performing, a perfect combination to be accompanying you on your magical journey. He has a playful sense of humor, which you will enjoy in his approach. Practitioners of the art will appreciate that he has meticulously referenced all the effects, endeavoring to give credit to the original creators of the ideas and methods used.

This book is full of secrets about how you can do astounding magic and about how to perform magic and become a skillful entertainer. I will close by telling you one of Bryan Miles's closely guarded secrets that will not be found elsewhere in this book: Bryan Miles is one of the nicest people you will ever meet— he goes out of his way to help other magicians and gives generously to the community. There, I believe, lies a hint for anyone who wants to be a successful magical entertainer.

Enjoy and have fun!

DAVID GORE
Director, College of Magic
December 2014

WELCOME TO THE WORLD OF MAGIC!

MAGIC IS ALL ABOUT MAKING THE IMPOSSIBLE BECOME POSSIBLE. THE ART OF THE MAGICIAN IS TO CREATE WONDER AND ASTONISHMENT—IF ONLY FOR A MOMENT IN TIME.

Look for this icon throughout for a "secret view" of the action.

WHAT IS THIS BOOK ALL ABOUT?

This book will equip you with practical effects that you can perform in real-world situations. No need to carry a special apparatus in your pocket everywhere you go; this book will prepare you with effects and techniques that will always have you ready to entertain and amaze your audience.

Threaded throughout this book are presentational tips on performing your magic effects; don't overlook them, for they will help you take your magic to the next level! You'll also find bite-sized pieces of information about famous magicians past and present—you can learn a lot from these masters of magic!

WHY?

The art of magic is a universal language and can be appreciated the world over. Almost everyone enjoys the amazement that comes with making the ordinary appear extraordinary.

ISN'T MAGIC HARD TO LEARN?

In this book you will learn to do magic for just about every occasion in your everyday life—from showing your friends magic at school to performing for your colleagues at the office. The magic effects in this book have been handpicked to get you up and performing in no time!

KINDS OF MAGIC

Magic is often divided into certain categories based upon the audience it is intended to be performed for. In this book, I categorize the magic effects according to the context or environment in which you may find yourself, such as out at a restaurant or perhaps attending a friend's birthday party.

THE BEGINNING!

WHEN YOU PERFORM MAGIC, IT WILL BE IMPORTANT THAT YOU CONTROL YOUR AUDIENCE'S ATTENTION. YOU WANT TO TAKE THEM ON A JOURNEY OF WONDER AND ASTONISHMENT, BUT YOU NEED TO SECRETLY GUIDE THEM. LET'S TURN THE TABLES AND EXPERIENCE WHAT IT'S LIKE TO BE AN AUDIENCE MEMBER.

Here I am holding a photograph of some dice. Answer this question before you read on: How many of these twelve dice are red?

Do you count seven? Congratulations! You are correct. Not that amazing, right? But what *is* amazing is that you most likely did not notice the following:

I mentioned there were twelve dice in total; there are actually fifteen.

All of the green dice are misnumbered with numbers that are incorrectly placed on a die.

One fingernail on my left hand is black.

This was your first lesson in magic. One of the skills a magician must use is that of controlling attention, often referred to as misdirection. Misdirection can be words or actions—or both. The question I asked you earlier was designed to point your attention toward one area. You were focused on one piece of information and neglected the other pieces of information.

Amazingly simple, but simply amazing—that is how easily our brains can be misled. Not only will magic entertain your audience, but it will also allow *you* to see how simplicity can create astonishment. Often the secrets behind the magic are simple and sometimes disappointing, but don't let this distract you. Magic is all about showmanship and entertaining your audience—the secrets are merely stepping stones toward that place we call wonder.

> **A LITTLE MAGIC CAN TAKE YOU A LONG WAY.**
> ROALD DAHL

CHAPTER 1

THE FOUNDATION

IN THIS CHAPTER, YOU WILL LEARN PLAYING CARD AND COIN ESSENTIALS TO HELP LAY A SOLID FOUNDATION FOR THE EFFECTS THAT FOLLOW.

To learn the effects in this book, it will be essential that you understand the basic terminology that magicians use. Selected effects will require you to handle playing cards and coins with a certain amount of skill. This chapter will lay a solid foundation for you, so make sure you don't skip it!

The next time you are handed a deck of cards you'll be able to display all the cards in a strikingly visual two-handed card spread, elegantly interweave the cards together in a stunning riffle shuffle, and secretly control your volunteer's free selection of a card.

The next time you are handed a coin you'll make it dance from finger to finger before making it vanish into thin air! Coins will no longer simply be currency, but rather they will become the very props you use to create close-up miracles—wherever you are!

THEORY: THE MAGICIAN IS AN ACTOR

If you want to be a good magician you do not have to pretend to be someone else, but you do have to be able to act. You will need to think about your appearance, what you say, and how you move. The manner in which you act depends largely on the environment you perform in as well as how many people you are performing for.

THE HAND

TO ACCURATELY LEARN THE EFFECTS IN THIS BOOK IT WILL BE ESSENTIAL THAT WE UNDERSTAND EACH OTHER AND USE THE SAME TERMINOLOGY. HAVE A LOOK BELOW AND FAMILIARIZE YOURSELF WITH THE PARTS OF THE HAND.

THE HAND:

1	Thumb
2	First finger
3	Second finger
4	Third finger
5	Fourth finger
6	Base of thumb
7	Palm
8	Palm up
9	Palm down

HISTORY: DEDI

An ancient Egyptian text known as the *Westcar Papyrus* describes a fictitious Egyptian magician known as Dedi. He was said to be 110 years old and gifted with magical powers. His most legendary act was decapitating a goose in front of King Khufu. He cast a magic spell and the goose's head was restored. The goose was heard cackling as it left the hall! The *Westcar Papyrus* is currently on display at the Egyptian Museum of Berlin.

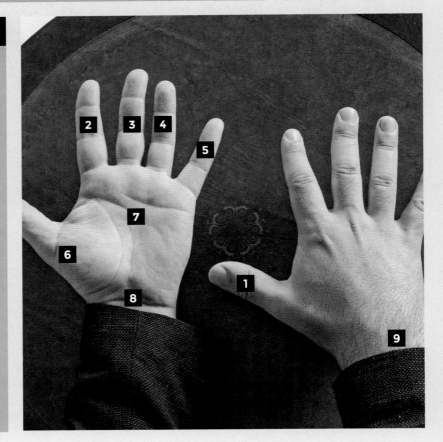

THE DECK OF CARDS

TO ACCOMPLISH THE EFFECTS AND SLEIGHTS INVOLVING CARDS, IT WILL BE IMPORTANT THAT YOU UNDERSTAND THE BASIC TERMINOLOGY. TAKE A LOOK BELOW AND FAMILIARIZE YOURSELF WITH THE PARTS OF A CARD.

THE DECK:

1 Ends
2 Sides
3 Top of deck
4 Bottom of deck
5 Face up
6 Face down
7 Index
8 Pip

THEORY: PLAYING CARD SYMBOLISM

There are different theories behind the symbolism in playing cards, but here is one theory worth noting.

The four suits—clubs, hearts, spades, and diamonds—represent the four seasons.

The thirteen cards in each suit represent the thirteen phases of the lunar cycle.

Fifty-two cards in a full deck represent the fifty-two weeks in a year.

If you add up all the spots (including a joker) you get 365—the number of days in a year.

MECHANIC'S GRIP AND BIDDLE GRIP

MECHANIC'S GRIP

The cards are held in the left hand with the thumb resting straight along the left side of the deck. The first finger is curled around the front of the deck with the other three fingers resting on the right side.

BIDDLE GRIP

The deck is held in the right hand from above with the thumb holding the end nearest to you. The second and third fingers hold the deck at the end furthest from you. The first finger is curled slightly and rests gently on top of the deck.

SPOTLIGHT: JEAN EUGÉNE ROBERT-HOUDIN

The French magician Jean Eugène Robert-Houdin (December 7, 1805–June 13, 1871) is widely known as the "Father of Modern Magic." He was the son of a watchmaker, and he himself became an expert watchmaker. He built his own mechanical inventions, such as a singing bird, a dancing tightrope walker, and an automaton that drew. His public performances were critically acclaimed and his shows elevated magic to a respectable level. Robert-Houdin passed away at the age of sixty-five. His home in Blois, France, is currently a museum and is open to the public.

CLASSIC TWO-HANDED SPREAD

MANY CARD EFFECTS INVOLVE A VOLUNTEER SELECTING A CARD. HERE IS A NEAT WAY TO OFFER THE VOLUNTEER A SELECTION. THE CARDS ARE SPREAD BETWEEN THE HANDS IN AN ELEGANT MANNER.

1 Hold the cards in the left-hand Mechanic's Grip (see page 14). The left thumb pushes a few cards off the top of the deck into the right hand.

2 The right hand receives and grips the spread of cards between the thumb and fingers. The left fingers and thumb push several cards over to the right, with the right fingers supporting from underneath.

3 Continue to spread cards by pushing with the left thumb. Spread the cards into a short line or arc.

MAGIC: FAN

1

2

Produce a stylish and beautiful display of cards.

Step 1: Hold the cards in your left hand with the end nearest to you in line with the third finger. The left thumb grips the cards firmly.

Step 2: The right first finger contacts the top end of the cards at the left corner. The right first finger rotates in a small semicircle while the cards are gripped firmly by the left thumb. The cards will swivel and spread automatically under the pad of the left thumb.

CUTTING THE CARDS

CUTTING THE CARDS ENTAILS DIVIDING THE DECK IN TWO AND PUTTING THE HALF THAT WAS ON THE BOTTOM ON TOP.

PERFORMANCE

1 Hold the deck of cards in the right hand with the Biddle Grip (see page 14). With your right first finger, lift half the cards off the deck at the top end (furthest away from you).

2 Rotate the lifted packet of cards to the left (they will pivot on your right thumb).

3 The left hand receives the lifted packet between the left thumb and first finger. Place the cards that are in your right hand on top to complete the cut.

MAGIC: CHARLIER CUT

This is a classy cut using only one hand.

PERFORMANCE:

Step 1: Hold the deck high up in the left hand at the tips of the fingers with the right thumb supporting one side of the deck.

Step 2: Release pressure from the right thumb and allow roughly half the deck to fall into the palm of the left hand.

Step 3: Curl the first finger under the deck and push the bottom packet up toward the left thumb.

Step 4: Let the bottom packet clear the top packet, which will fall.

Step 5: Close your left thumb and fingers together to complete the cut.

OVERHAND SHUFFLE

ONE OF THE MOST COMMONLY USED SHUFFLES IS KNOWN AS THE OVERHAND SHUFFLE; LET'S LEARN HOW TO DO IT PROPERLY.

PERFORMANCE

1 Hold the deck in the right hand as shown, with the four right fingers on the outer end and the thumb at the inner end. The deck should be at a slight angle to the ground.

2 The left fingers approach the deck from underneath and the left thumb rests on the uppermost card. Ease the grip with the right thumb and first finger, allowing roughly the 10 uppermost cards to fall into the cradle of the left hand. The left thumb applies pressure on top of these cards.

3 Repeat this action, sliding small packets of cards from the top of the right-hand packet and allowing them to fall on top of the left-hand packet. Repeat this action until all the cards have been transferred from the right hand into the left hand.

RIFFLE
SHUFFLE

THIS IS AN ELEGANT AND PROFESSIONAL-LOOKING SHUFFLE THAT MAKES USE OF A TABLE SURFACE.

PERFORMANCE

1 Start with the deck facedown on the table. Cut off roughly half the deck and place it to the right of the bottom packet.

2 Both hands will now mirror each other. With the thumbs of both hands, lift up the packets by the sides closest to you (the thumbs are positioned just off center).

3 Both first fingers rest curled on top of the packets while the second and third fingers hold the opposite sides. Both pinkies are positioned on the outer end of each packet.

4 Allow the cards to riffle off both thumbs, and at the same time bring the packets together so the cards' corners overlap. Riffle the cards evenly until all the cards are woven together.

5 Change your grip as you move both hands together. Use your little fingers to help keep the deck square.

HINDU FORCE

SEVERAL EFFECTS IN THIS BOOK WILL REQUIRE YOU TO GET YOUR VOLUNTEER TO SELECT A PLAYING CARD. DESPITE THE CHOICE APPEARING FREE AND FAIR, YOU WILL SECRETLY BE CONTROLLING THE CHOSEN CARD. THIS IS KNOWN AS *FORCING* A CARD. THERE ARE MANY WAYS TO FORCE A PLAYING CARD—LET'S LEARN THREE EFFECTIVE ONES.

PERFORMANCE

1 The card you will force should be on the bottom of the deck. In this example it is the Seven of Hearts.

2 Hold the deck at the tips of the left fingers with the first finger at the end of the deck furthest away from you. Hold the deck as high up in the fingertips as possible.

TAKE IT FURTHER:
The same procedure can be used to legitimately shuffle a deck of cards. By completing steps 1 to 4 until the entire deck is used up, you are executing what is known as a Hindu Shuffle.

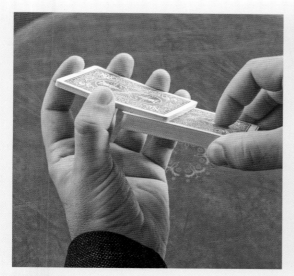

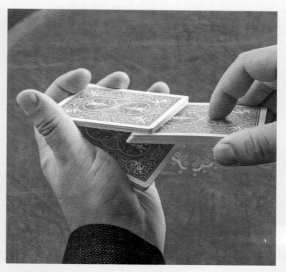

3 The right hand approaches and takes roughly the bottom three-quarters of the deck away. The right first finger is curled on top, the right thumb on the side closest to you with the second and third fingers on the opposite side.

4 Let the packet of cards in the left hand fall to the left palm. The right hand returns and the left fingers and thumb grip a small packet of cards from the top of the deck. Let these cards fall onto the cards below.

5 Continue this procedure and the bottom card in the right hand will always remain the same. Ask your volunteer to say "Stop!" at any point during this shuffle. When she says, "Stop!" you show the bottom card of the right-hand packet—this is your force card. Drop the entire right-hand packet on top of the cards in the left hand to finish.

CRISS-CROSS FORCE

THE FOLLOWING FORCE IS DECEPTIVELY SIMPLE, BUT RELIES ON *TIME MISDIRECTION* —THAT IS, ALLOWING A CERTAIN AMOUNT OF TIME TO PASS AFTER EXECUTING A MOVE; THE VOLUNTEER WILL THEN BE UNABLE TO RECALL THE EXACT SEQUENCE OF EVENTS.

PERFORMANCE

1 The force card is on top of the deck.

2 Ask the volunteer to cut the deck into two packets, side by side. (You must secretly keep track of which packet is the original top half.)

3 Pick up the packet that was the original bottom half of the deck and place it across the top packet.

4 Now execute some time misdirection by talking to the volunteer or reciting your patter (see page 35). The volunteer will forget the true orientation of the cards. You now pick up the top packet of cards and offer the card that was supposedly cut to—in reality, this is your force card.

SLIP FORCE

HERE IS ONE FINAL METHOD FOR FORCING A CARD. IT'S DONE
ENTIRELY IN THE HANDS AND IS EXTREMELY DECEPTIVE.

PERFORMANCE

1 The force card is on top of the deck.

2 The deck is held in the left hand in the Mechanic's Grip (see page 14). Curl the first finger under the deck and use the left thumb to riffle (see page 20) the corner of the cards from top to bottom. Ask the volunteer to call "Stop!" as you riffle down the corner of the cards.

3 The right hand now removes all the riffled-off cards by lifting straight up. The left hand's second, third, and fourth fingers keep contact and pressure on the top card (your force card). The right hand continues to remove the cards and the force card falls flush onto the bottom half.

4 The right hand taps its packet on the bottom half of the deck and the left hand moves forward to offer the top card to the volunteer. This will appear to be the card that was stopped at.

FINGER PALM

IT'S TIME FOR YOU TO LEARN SOME SLEIGHT OF HAND THAT WILL ENABLE YOU TO PERFORM DAZZLING MAGIC EFFECTS. BEAR IN MIND THAT THESE MOVES WILL TAKE PRACTICE TO GET RIGHT, BUT THEY WILL BE WELL WORTH THE EFFORT—AND THEY ARE FUN TO LEARN!

PERFORMANCE

The following grip is extremely versatile and will allow you to secretly hold and hide a coin in your hand.

1 Place the coin against the base of the right hand second and third fingers. The fingers curl in slightly and the coin is held in place by the creases in the skin.

2 Make sure there are no gaps between the fingers. It should appear from the front as though your hand is not holding anything.

Try the same grip with different objects other than a coin:

THEORY: PRACTICE

It is important that you practice and rehearse properly before you perform any of the effects in this book for the public. A good way to learn is to read through the effects step by step, from start to finish. Once you have read the entire effect, start to practice step by step with the props in hand. Use a mirror to practice and get the moves natural. Once you feel confident, stop using the mirror and focus on imagining the audience in front of you. It also helps to rename the word *practice* to *play*—you should want to play as much as you can!

CLASSIC PALM

HERE IS ANOTHER EXCEPTIONALLY USEFUL AND MULTIPURPOSE GRIP TO LEARN. IT IS IMPORTANT THAT YOU HOLD THE ITEM WITH A LIGHT TOUCH—YOUR HAND SHOULD REMAIN IN A NATURAL POSITION.

PERFORMANCE

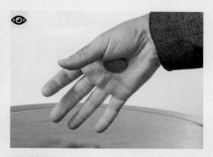

1 Place the coin on the tips of the right hand's second and third fingers.

2 Turn the right hand palm down, but keep the fingers parallel to the ground. This brings the coin directly below the palm of the right hand. Use the third finger to push the coin up into the palm of the right hand.

3 The coin should be held in the palm by gently pushing the edges between the pad of the thumb and the skin on the opposite edge of the coin.

4 The coin can be held naturally in Classic Palm without detection.

5 When both hands are naturally resting on a table, they should mirror each other. From the front it should appear as though your hands are not holding anything.

HISTORY:
THE DISCOVERIE OF WITCHCRAFT **BY REGINALD SCOT**

The Discoverie of Witchcraft was printed in 1584 and is considered to be one of the first published materials on magic. In it, Englishman Reginald Scot set out to explain the difference between magic and witchcraft. The book attempted to demonstrate how certain miraculous feats were accomplished by sleight of hand and not by the Devil. It was declared heretical and King James I ordered the book to be burned. Some copies survived and serve as great historical records.

FRENCH DROP

HERE IS A CLASSIC METHOD TO MAKE A COIN VANISH. THIS SLEIGHT SHOULD IDEALLY BE USED IN CONJUNCTION WITH ANOTHER EFFECT AND NOT AS AN EFFECT ON ITS OWN.

PERFORMANCE

1 Hold the coin in the palm-up right hand at the very tips of the first finger with the right thumb on the side closest to you.

2 The left hand simulates taking the coin with all four fingers over the top of the coin with the left thumb underneath.

3 As the left fingers close over the coin, drop the coin into the palm of the right hand. The coin will naturally fall into the Finger Palm position in the right hand (see page 28).

Try the same sleight with different objects other than a coin:

4 The left hand continues to simulate grabbing the coin at the fingertips and moves up and to the left. Your eyes should follow the movement of the left hand as your right hand drops naturally to your side.

5 Make a gentle squeezing action with the left hand and slowly open the fingers to reveal the coin has vanished.

BOBO SWITCH

THIS SLEIGHT WILL ENABLE YOU TO SWITCH ONE COIN FOR ANOTHER AND IS NEEDED FOR THE EFFECT IN THE "STREET MAGIC" CHAPTER CALLED "COIN BEND."

PERFORMANCE

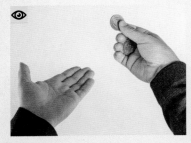

1 The coin that will be switched is in the right hand Finger Palm position (see page 28). The other coin is displayed at the fingertips of the right hand.

2 The left hand is held out flat with the palm up. You will now apparently toss the coin at the fingertips into the left hand. In reality, the right second and third fingers extend and cover the coin at the fingertips and the coin in the Finger Palm is allowed to fall into the left hand.

3 As the left hand closes over the switched coin, the right hand moves the original coin into Finger Palm position.

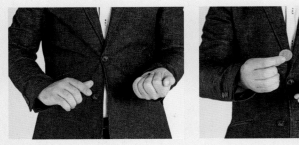

Try the same sleight with different objects other than a coin. You could do a color-changing sharpener or color-changing glue cap.

4 From the audience's view it looks as though you merely tossed the coin from the right fingertips into the open left hand.

MAGIC: COIN ROLL

Make a coin gracefully dance across your knuckles!

PERFORMANCE:

Step 1: Curl the right hand with the fingers together and parallel to the floor. Balance a coin on the tip of the right thumb.

Step 2: Move the right thumb against the first finger so the coin is flipped 90 degrees onto its side.

Step 3: The thumb releases pressure and the coin is balanced on top of the first finger. At the same time, raise the second finger just enough to clip the coin's edge. Bring the second finger down while raising the third finger. This will allow the coin to roll across the back of the second finger.

Step 4: Repeat this process until the coin rests on the fourth finger. Move the right thumb under the hand and transfer the coin onto the edge of the thumb. The thumb now brings the coin back to the starting position. You can now repeat the coin roll sequence again.

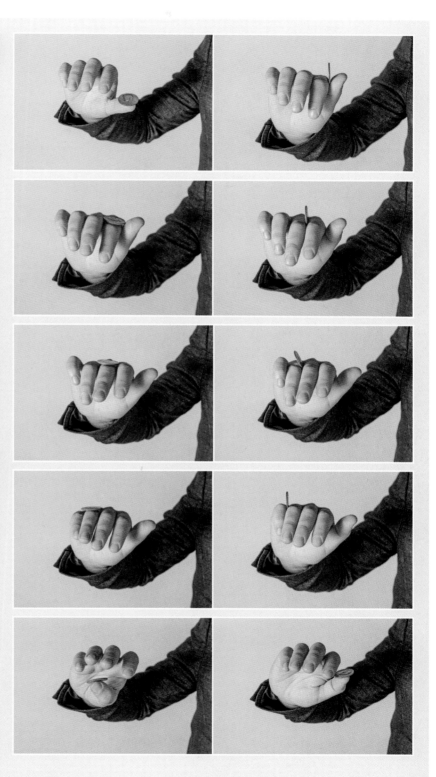

> **ASTONISHMENT IS NOT AN EMOTION THAT'S CREATED. IT'S AN EXISTING STATE THAT'S REVEALED.**
> PAUL HARRIS

CHAPTER 2

MAGIC IN THE CLASSROOM

YOU ARE SITTING IN THE CLASSROOM OR LECTURE HALL JUST WAITING FOR THE LESSON TO END.

It's been a long day of consuming knowledge and learning, but that is about to change—time to captivate your classmates with some moments of astonishment and wonder. You reach for some items of stationery and proceed to perform mind-blowing magic for them. The lackluster lesson is forgotten for a moment as you shatter your classmates' perception of reality—the true power of magic.

How about making a sharpener vanish into thin air? Or magically changing the color of a pencil or crayon? Amaze your classmates with your eraser that has mysterious superpowers!

This chapter will prove that you can bring magic to school and make the classroom or lecture hall your stage!

THEORY: PATTER

Patter is what you say while performing an effect. Your patter should sound natural and can be used to distract or entertain your audience. Some effects will require you to simply talk through what you are doing—this is known as explanatory patter. Other effects might require you to come up with a short story to engage your audience.

COLOR SENSE

YOU ARE ABLE TO CORRECTLY SENSE THE COLOR OF CRAYONS BEHIND YOUR BACK—WITHOUT LOOKING! THIS GIVES ANOTHER MEANING TO THE SAYING *"DO YOU HAVE EYES IN THE BACK OF YOUR HEAD?!"*

REQUIREMENTS:

3 different-colored crayons

PREPARATION

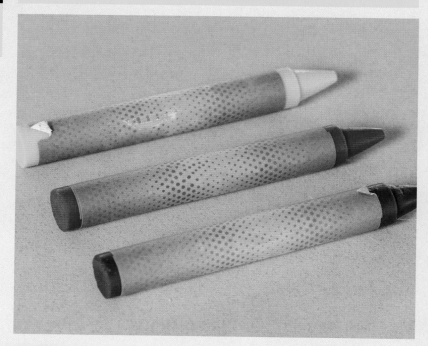

1 Mark each crayon in a unique way, so that you can tell which crayon is which by simply feeling them. These marks must be subtle and almost invisible to your audience.

Nick one crayon on the bottom with your fingernail or scissors, and make a nick on the top of the second crayon. The third one is marked in the middle by making a small tear in the paper. Make sure you know and remember which mark corresponds with which color.

1 Display the three different colored crayons and hand them to your volunteer. Turn your back toward the volunteer and instruct him to randomly place the crayons into your hands, which you put behind your back.

2 Turn and face the volunteer. Ask him to call out any one of the colors. Feel for the mark that matches the color called.

3 Dramatically reveal the correct color crayon! You can do the same effect one more time with the remaining two crayons behind your back.

What about using other objects? Colored pencils could be used—you mark two according to the sharpness of the tip of their leads; one is very sharp and one is blunt. The final colored pencil could be slightly shorter than the other two.

TAKE IT FURTHER

What about using other objects? Colored pencils could be used—you mark two according to the sharpness of the tip of their leads; one is very sharp and one is blunt. The final colored pencil could be slightly shorter than the other two.

MAGICAL PENDULUM

AN ERASER WITH SUPERPOWERS! YOUR ERASER ACTS AS A PENDULUM AND CAN MAGICALLY DIVINE MALE CELEBRITIES FROM FEMALE CELEBRITIES!

REQUIREMENTS:

An eraser

Piece of string

Paper

Pencil

PREPARATION

1 Cut the string to about the length of your arm and tie one end of the string around your eraser. You now have a magical divining device! Tear the sheet of paper into eight equal pieces. It is important that you tear the paper; do not use scissors.

2 When you tear the paper into eight equal pieces, the middle four pieces will have three rough edges and one smooth edge—these go to your four friends writing *male* celebrity names. The four outer corner pieces will have two rough edges and two smooth edges—these go to the four friends writing *female* celebrity names.

 1 Hand eight of your friends one of the torn-off pieces of paper each. Instruct four of your friends to write down the name of a famous *male* celebrity and the other four friends to write down the name of a famous *female* celebrity. These celebrities could be anyone from famous movie stars to sports figures. Make sure you hand the correct papers to the correct friends!

2 One of your friends gathers all the papers with the names facing down and mixes them. She then spreads the papers on the table.

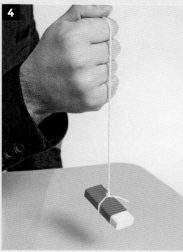

3 Grab hold of your string with the eraser hanging at the bottom and hold it slightly above the papers on the table. Explain that the eraser will swing *back and forth* over names that are male celebrities, but will *circle* over the names with female celebrities.

4 Hold the string between your thumb and first fingers and make the eraser swing or circle over each paper, according to which paper you secretly can identify. Thanks to your secret marking system you can state whether the paper has a male or female name written on it! As you announce each paper, turn it over to show you are right.

TAKE IT FURTHER: Why only celebrity names? What about using animals vs. plants; countries vs. cars . . . you name it.

COLOR-CHANGING PENCIL

ATTEMPT TO MAKE AN ERASER DISAPPEAR; INSTEAD, THE COLOR OF YOUR PENCIL CHANGES RIGHT UNDER YOUR CLASSMATE'S NOSE!

REQUIREMENTS:

An eraser

2 different colored pencils (red and green are perfect)

PREPARATION

Tuck the green pencil halfway under your right collar; you will stand with your left side facing your friend so she will not see it partially sticking out.

PERFORMANCE

1 Stand with your left side facing your friend. Place the eraser on your open left palm and in your right hand hold the red pencil near the end.

2 Explain to your friend that you will attempt to make the eraser vanish by using the magic word "Go!" Close your left-hand fingers, concealing the eraser.

3 Begin to bend your right arm at the elbow and bring your hand with the red pencil up so it is level with your right ear. This is going to be your magical gesture. Bring your right hand down and tap the back of your closed left hand with the end of the red pencil. As you do this, count out loud, "One!"

4 Do this exact action again as you count, "Two!"

5 Proceed to do the same action a third time, but this time place the red pencil behind your ear and leave it there. In the same movement grab the green pencil out from your collar and continue to bring your right hand down to tap the now green pencil crayon on your closed left fingers. As you do this say, "Go!

6 Open your left hand to reveal the eraser has not vanished, but instead the pencil has changed color from red to green!

7 On this offbeat moment, hand the green pencil to your friend to examine; at the same time, secretly drop the eraser into your left pocket. Keep your left hand in a closed fist and retrieve the green pencil

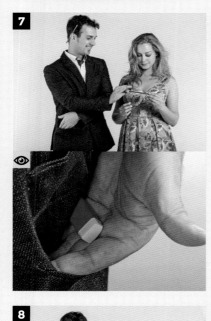

8 Proceed with the same actions from step 3, except this time the eraser really vanishes!

9 Hand the green pencil to the volunteer again and secretly move the red pencil from behind your right ear to inside your collar to finish.

PERPLEXING PAPER RINGS

CHALLENGE YOUR FRIENDS TO CUT A LOOP OF PAPER INTO TWO SEPARATE LOOPS—IT SOUNDS SO SIMPLE, YET THEY ALL END UP WITH DIFFERENT RESULTS.

REQUIREMENTS:

A pair of scissors

Glue

3 pieces of paper

PREPARATION

1 Cut three strips of paper each approximately 20 by 1¼ inches (60 by 3 cm). Glue the ends of one strip together to form a loop.

2 Do the same with the second loop, but before you glue the ends, give the paper two twists (turn it over and then over again).

3 Give the third strip of paper one twist.

4 You now have three loops of paper that appear to be the same, but when you cut them down the middle they will produce very different results!

PERFORMANCE

2

1 Display the three loops of paper and hand two friends each one of the loops. Make sure to keep the loop that has no twists.

2 Explain to your volunteers that you will have a competition. You show them that all they have to do is cut down the middle of their loop of paper and produce two separate loops. You demonstrate this with your loop. Tell them that is all they have to do in order to win.

3

3 Count to three and have them begin to cut their loops. Neither of them will be able to copy you—one will end up with two loops of paper linked and the other will have one large loop!

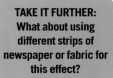

TAKE IT FURTHER: What about using different strips of newspaper or fabric for this effect?

SHARPENER VANISH

VISUALLY MAKE A SHARPENER VANISH WITH ONE HAND WHILE SEATED AT YOUR DESK—NO SLEEVES!

PERFORMANCE

1 You need to be seated at your desk or table. The sharpener is in front of you near the center of the desk. You will pretend to slide and pick up the sharpener, but in reality it will fall into your lap.

2 Turn your right hand palm down with your fingers closed and cover the sharpener. Your hand is almost flat on the desk. Keep contact with the desk and slide your right hand toward yourself as you simulate picking the sharpener up. The sharpener will slide under the fingers of your right hand.

In order for your audience to truly suspend their disbelief, they must sense a magical moment. Magicians often use a magic wand or magical gesture to *make* the magic happen. Think about where the magical moments in your effects are and make sure you communicate them effectively.

4 Make a magical gesture and slowly open the fingers of your right hand to show the sharpener has vanished!

TAKE IT FURTHER:
The same technique can be used to make your eraser vanish or anything small enough to be concealed behind your four fingers.

3 When your hand reaches the edge of the desk, let the sharpener fall secretly into your lap. Keep your fingers together and act as though you are still holding the sharpener. Your right hand rotates through 180 degrees and is brought forward.

MIND TAPPED

YOUR FRIEND THINKS OF AN OBJECT; YOU TAP EACH ITEM AS HE SPELLS THE NAME OF THE OBJECT IN HIS MIND—AND YOU CORRECTLY DIVINE HIS THOUGHTS.

REQUIREMENTS:

Sharpener

Pin

Stapler

Pencil

Ruler

Glue

Scissors

Calculator

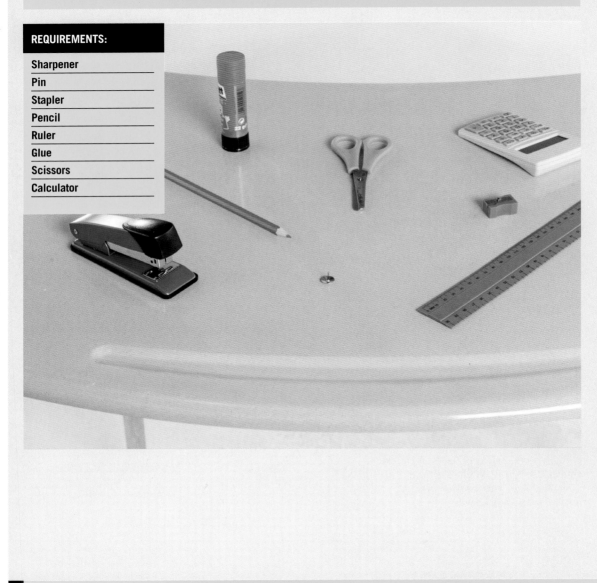

PREPARATION

Each object you use has a different number of letters in its name. You will need to remember how many letters there are in the name of each object.

Calculator	10 letters
Sharpener	9 letters
Scissors	8 letters
Stapler	7 letters
Pencil	6 letters
Ruler	5 letters
Glue	4 letters
Pin	3 letters

PERFORMANCE

1 Place all eight objects on the table in front of you and tap each object as you name it out loud to your friend. For example, say, "pin," "glue," and so forth.

2 Ask your friend to think of one of the objects. Explain that you will tap the objects one by one and he is to silently spell to himself the name of the object, in time to your tapping—one letter for each tap. Tell him to stop you on the last letter.

3 Tap any two objects for the first two taps; thereafter, follow the order of the number of letters in the object's name, starting with the pin (three letters), then glue (four letters), and so on. When your friend says, "Stop!" you will be pointing at his secretly thought-of object!

It is possible to use other objects; simply make sure they have the right number of letters in the name.

VANISHING AND APPEARING GLUE CAP

YOUR GLUE STICK CAP DISAPPEARS AND REAPPEARS— UNDER YOUR ARM AND BACK ON YOUR THUMB IN LIGHTNING SPEED! WHO KNOWS WHERE IT WILL JUMP NEXT?

REQUIREMENTS:

A glue stick cap

PREPARATION

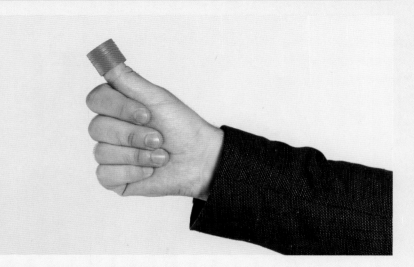

1 Hold your right hand in a fist with your thumb pointing up. Place the glue cap on your right thumb.

2 Bend your thumb in and grip the glue cap in your curled fingers. Then, remove your thumb, leaving the glue cap in your closed fist.

3 By reversing this move you can place the glue cap back onto your right thumb.

MAGIC: ALPHA-BET!

Learn to say the alphabet backwards with rapid speed!

PREPARATION:

Step 1: By grouping the letters of the alphabet together you will be able to memorize them easier. Group the letters as follows:

zyx, wvu, ts, rq, pon, mlk, jihg, fed, cba

Step 2: Memorize the letter groups. This way you only have nine pieces of information to memorize and not twenty-six individual letters. With some practice this sequence will be stuck in your head!

1 Hold your right hand in a fist with your thumb pointing up. Place the glue cap on your right thumb. Pretend to grab the glue cap off your right thumb with your left hand, but in reality execute the secret move. It will appear as though the glue cap is now in your closed left hand.

2 Draw attention to your closed left hand as you pretend to place the glue cap under your right arm. Your left hand can now be shown empty as you bring your right arm down as though it were holding the glue cap against your body.

3 Make a magical gesture with your left hand and bring your right arm up above your head to show the glue cap has vanished! At the same time, while your right hand is slightly out of sight behind your shoulder, execute the secret move again. Quickly bring your right hand back into view and it will appear as though the glue cap has appeared back on your right thumb!

WHICH HAND?

CORRECTLY GUESS WHICH HAND YOUR FRIEND IS HIDING HER ERASER IN—99.9 PERCENT OF THE TIME!

REQUIREMENTS:

An eraser

MAGIC: THE MAGIC OF THE NUMBER 9

Show off your lightning calculations with this fascinating math tip!

PERFORMANCE:
Step 1: Here's how you can multiply by 9 by just using your fingers. Hold both your hands palm up in front of you. In your head number them 1 to 10, starting with your left thumb.

Step 2: Simply bend down the finger of whichever number you wish to multiply by 9. However many fingers are left standing on each side will be your answer. For example, to multiply 4 by 9, bend finger number 4 down and count the fingers to the left and right of it. There will be 3 on your left and 6 on your right—the answer is 36! Any multiple up to 10 will work!

PERFORMANCE

1 Place an eraser into your friend's hand.

2 Turn your back and instruct her to place the eraser into either hand, close her fist, and hold it high above her head. She must count to ten out loud and then repeat the magical phrase "Which hand?" five times.

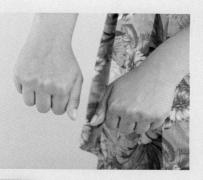

3 Instruct her to lower her hand and hold both closed fists in front of her. Turn around and tell her not to say which hand contains the eraser. Secretly compare her hands; one will be slightly paler because the blood has drained from the hand while it was above her head. This is the hand that contains the eraser.

4 Dramatically use your hands to sense which one of her hands contains the eraser. Finish by pointing to the hand that holds the eraser.

TAKE IT FURTHER: Other objects could be used, such as a pencil sharpener or pen cap.

> **CHILDREN SEE MAGIC BECAUSE THEY LOOK FOR IT.**
> CHRISTOPHER MOORE

CHAPTER 3

BIRTHDAY MAGIC

WE ALL HAVE THEM, AND EVERY YEAR THEY OFFER THE OPPORTUNITY FOR A FUN CELEBRATION—I'M TALKING ABOUT BIRTHDAYS!

When we are young we love them, and as we get older we hope that they will start to slow down. Whether you are celebrating someone else's birthday or your own, you will now be the life of the party.

Imagine presenting a birthday card that predicts the future! Or how about blowing out a lit candle only to find that it has completely vanished into thin air? Birthday parties will never be the same again; expect to be invited to every birthday party in town—your magic effects will get people talking about the party for years to come.

In this chapter you will learn to perform magic effects that have a strong emotional connection and will complement the birthday party perfectly. The magic words are "Hip, hip, hooray!"

THEORY: MAKE IT INTERESTING

Storytelling can be a powerful way to draw your audience in and make a somewhat ordinary effect appear more entertaining.

THEORY: PERSONALITY EXTENSION

It is important that you put your own personality into your performances. Decide on what style of presentation you wish to pursue—are you a funny person, or do you perhaps like to be serious? Extend yourself into the effects you perform and your audience will be more likely to warm to you.

PHONE-NOMENAL BIRTHDAY

YOU CALL YOUR FRIEND ON THE PHONE—CONTROL HIS MIND AND PREDICT WHICH CARD HE WILL LEAVE FACE UP!

REQUIREMENTS:

9 cardboard cards

An envelope

Paper

A coin

PREPARATION

1 Print out nine cards with different holidays on them. Four of these holidays should be printed in black and white and the other five should be in color (make sure the "Happy Birthday" card is printed in color).

2 On a piece of paper print, "I predict the only card remaining face up will be the 'HAPPY BIRTHDAY' card!" Seal this paper in an envelope.

2

MERRY CHRISTMAS	HAPPY HANNUKAH	HAPPY SAINT PATRICK'S DAY
HAPPY VALENTINE'S DAY	HAPPY BIRTHDAY	HAPPY NEW YEAR
HAPPY EASTER	HAPPY ANNIVERSARY	HAPPY INDEPENDENCE DAY

1 A few days before your friend's birthday, give him the sealed envelope, nine cards, and coin. Tell him you will call him on the phone on his birthday.

2 On the day of his birthday, give your friend a call and tell him to lay out the nine cards in three rows of three. The "Happy Birthday" card should be in the middle, the other four cards with colored frames at the corners, and the four cards with black frames in between.

3 Instruct your friend to place the coin on any holiday card with a black frame. Explain that you are going to instruct him to make certain "hops." A "hop" means moving the coin to the next card above, below, or on either side, but not diagonally.

4 You will now give your friend the following instructions. It is a specific formula, but make it seem like you are making it up on the spot.

1. Start with the coin on any card with a black frame. Turn over "Happy Independence Day".

2. Hop four times. Your coin did not land on "Happy St. Patrick's Day"; turn that card over.

3. Hop seven times. Your coin did not land on "Happy New Year"; turn it over.

4. Hop seven times. You are not on "Merry Christmas"; turn it over.

5. Hop once. You are not on "Happy Anniversary"; turn it over.

6. Hop twice. Your coin did not land on "Happy Hannukah"; turn that card over.

7. Hop five times. You are not on "Happy Easter"; turn it over.

8. Hop three times. You are not on "Happy Valentine's Day"; turn it over.

5

5 After this procedure the only card left facing up will be the "Happy Birthday" card. Instruct your friend to open the sealed envelope. He will be amazed that your prediction has come true. Don't forget to wish him a magical birthday!

HISTORY: EGYPTIAN HALL JOHN NEVIL MASKELYNE AND DAVID DEVANT

The Egyptian Hall was a large performance venue built in ancient Egyptian style in Piccadilly, London. By the end of the nineteenth century, the Egyptian Hall had become known as England's Home of Mystery. John Nevil Maskelyne and David Devant were some of the famous magicians who presented their acts there. In 1905 the building was demolished and Maskelyne relocated to St George's Hall in London.

BIRTHDAY CARD FOR YOU!

A SECRETLY CHOSEN CARD IS FOUND BY SPELLING THE BIRTHDAY PERSON'S DATE OF BIRTH! AS A KICKER, THREE CHOCOLATES APPEAR TO PROVE YOU KNEW THE CARD ALL ALONG.

REQUIREMENTS:

A deck of cards

3 small heart-shaped chocolates

Styrofoam cup

PREPARATION

1 Start with the force card (the Three of Hearts) on the bottom of the deck and place three small heart-shaped chocolates in the bottom of the Styrofoam cup.

2 Place the card case on top of the Styrofoam cup.

1 Perform an Overhand Shuffle (see page 18), but drop the final few cards back on the bottom of the deck; this will keep your force card (the Three of Hearts) on the bottom. Perform the Hindu Force, but after the volunteer says "Stop!" and has noted his card, continue the Hindu Force until all the cards are used. This will put the force card on top of the deck.

2 Pick up the card case off the cup and place it on the table. Place the deck in the Styrofoam cup facing the audience. The deck should stick partially out of the cup. As you place the deck into the cup, push the top card far down into the cup. This will keep the card down until you need it.

3 Ask the volunteer for his birthday and explain you will spell it out using one card for each letter. Take cards from the back of the deck (leaving the force card down in the cup and taking the cards underneath it); let the audience see each card as you drop it on the table. When you reach the last letter, pull out the force card.

4 As an entertaining kicker to the effect, take the deck out of the cup and dump out the three heart-shaped chocolates on the table—three hearts!

SKETCH TO LIFE

YOU SKETCH A COIN AND CAST A MAGIC SPELL—THE DRAWING TURNS INTO A REAL COIN!

REQUIREMENTS:

2 identical sheets of colored paper

1 small piece of paper

A pencil

A coin

PREPARATION

 1 Fold two sheets of colored paper into nine identical squares.

2 Glue the two papers back to back so that they are joined by the center square only.

 3 Place the coin into the middle of one sheet and fold it up around the coin. Now fold the other sheet up and you will have a small packet of folded paper.

PERFORMANCE

SPOTLIGHT: JUSTIN WILLMAN

Justin Willman is an American magician, actor, and TV personality. He began performing at the age of twelve after breaking both his arms trying to ride a bicycle while wearing rollerblades. The doctor recommended that Justin learn card tricks to help with dexterity rehabilitation. He currently performs regularly at The Magic Castle in Los Angeles, California, and tours across the United States with his one-man show.

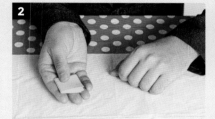

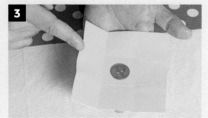

1 Hold the packet of folded paper with the packet containing the coin underneath. Unfold the top sheet and instruct the volunteer to draw a coin on the small piece of paper. Place this drawing in the middle of the open sheet.

2 Fold the open sheet up around the drawing and hold the package of folded paper in your right hand with the palm up. Turn your right hand palm down as you place the package into your palm-up left hand (secretly turning the package over).

3 Instruct the volunteer to wave her right index finger over the folded package. Unfold the package to reveal the drawing has turned into a real coin!

IMPOSSIBLE BIRTHDAY CARD PREDICTION

YOUR FRIEND OPENS HER BIRTHDAY CARD TO FIND YOU PREDICTED HER CHOSEN PLAYING CARD!

REQUIREMENTS:

A deck of cards

A birthday card

Envelope

PREPARATION

HAPPY BIRTHDAY!

Warmest thoughts and friendliest wishes for your happiest birthday yet.

ENJOY THE DAY

YOUR BIRTHDAY CARD WILL BE THE SEVEN OF HEARTS!

1 Inside the birthday card write your prediction, which reads, "Your birthday card will be the SEVEN OF HEARTS!" Don't forget to include your other birthday wishes in the card, too! Seal the birthday card inside an envelope and place the Seven of Hearts underneath the envelope.

2 Position the envelope with the card underneath near the edge of the table closest to you.

Make sure you handle your props as naturally as possible. Your audience might become suspicious if you begin to handle your props with too much care. Handle your props openly and freely, and you can even let your audience examine some of them.

 Have the birthday person shuffle the deck of cards. While she shuffles the deck, pick up the envelope with the Seven of Hearts hidden underneath.

 Instruct the birthday person to deal cards facedown into a pile on the table. Explain that she can stop dealing the cards at any point.

 As soon as she stops dealing cards, drop the envelope onto the pile dealt on the table.

4 Instruct her to open the envelope and read the message written in the birthday card.

 Now get her to turn over the card she stopped at . . . it is the Seven of Hearts.

CARD IN BALLOON

THE VOLUNTEER'S CHOSEN CARD APPEARS INSIDE THE BIRTHDAY BALLOON!

PREPARATION

1 Place the duplicate force card (in this example, the Three of Hearts) inside the blue balloon. The easiest way to do this is to lightly bend the card in half and then insert it through the neck of the balloon. Once inside, unroll it.

2 Inflate the blue balloon, tie the neck into a knot, and tie a string onto the end. Do the same with the red balloon.

3 Take any card from the deck (in this example it is the Jack of Spades) and trim 1/16 inch (1 mm) off the short end. Take the Three of Hearts and apply glue to the face of the bottom third (colored black for explanatory purposes), then stick it to the Jack of Spades along the untrimmed end.

4 Once dry, place this prepared double card in the center of the deck.

Try not to state the obvious when performing. Your audience can often see what you are doing and if you begin to overstate something, it will arouse suspicion and put the wrong ideas into the viewers' minds. It can also make your performance dull and not entertaining.

1 Display the balloons by holding one in each hand. Ask the volunteer to point to one of the balloons. If she points to the blue one, hand her the balloon. If she points to the red one, instruct her to pop the balloon with the pin. Either way, she is left with the blue balloon to hold.

2 Hold the deck of cards in your left hand and use your right first and second fingers to riffle (see page 20) up the edge of the deck. Starting at the bottom, begin slowly riffling and ask the volunteer to call, "Stop!" Time your riffle carefully and the cards will automatically stop at the prepared double card. Ask the volunteer to remember this card.

3 You now make your magical gesture over the deck of cards and begin to cleanly drop cards onto the table one by one to show that her card has vanished from the deck! (The gimmicked card will hide the force card.)

4 Hand the volunteer the pin and instruct her to pop the blue balloon; the duplicate force card will fall to the ground . . . and so will your volunteer's jaw!

BIRTHDAY CARD TRANSFORMATION

YOU SHOW A MINI BIRTHDAY CARD WITH THE INCORRECT BIRTHDAY AGE. USING YOUR MAGICAL POWERS, YOU CHANGE THE CARD TO THE CORRECT AGE!

REQUIREMENTS:

Electrical tape

2 different colored sheets of cardstock

Rubber cement

Scissors

Ruler

Pencil

PREPARATION

1 Measure and draw three rectangles approximately 6 by 3 inches (15 by 7.5 cm) onto one sheet of cardstock. Cut out the rectangles.

2 Join the rectangles together with strips of electrical tape. The tape will act as a hinge, allowing each rectangle to fold over. Put tape on the joins on the back of the rectangles, and finally along the two short sides.

3 Now make a concertina fold as shown and push the wallet flat on the table.

4 Cut two small rectangles approximately 2 by 3 inches (5 by 7.5 cm). Design two almost identical "Happy Birthday" cards—one has the incorrect age of the birthday person, and the other has the age he will be turning. Place the card with the correct birthday age between the two flaps of the wallet furthest away from you; between the opposite flaps place the incorrect birthday card. Use rubber cement to hold them in place.

1 Display the wallet in your right hand, open it, and show the incorrect birthday card.

2 Once your friend notices that the card displays the incorrect age, close the wallet and place it in your left hand (subtly turning it over in the process). Pretend to act really embarrassed and offer to try some magic to fix the situation.

3 Ask your friend to wave his hand over the wallet and say the magic words. Open the wallet to reveal the age has transformed into the correct age!

MIND-READING SPECTACLES

THE BIRTHDAY PERSON PUTS ON A PAIR OF GLASSES AND CORRECTLY DIVINES A SECRETLY CHOSEN PLAYING CARD.

REQUIREMENTS:

A pair of wide-rimmed sunglasses

A dry erase marker

Deck of cards

TIP

The only way for this effect to be ruined is if the volunteer spills the beans and tells the audience that the word was written on the sunglasses. Treat your volunteer with respect and he will most likely play along with you!

PREPARATION

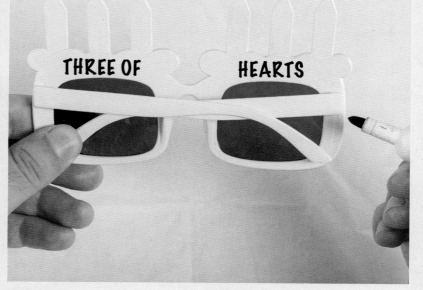

1 Use the dry erase marker to write the name of your force card on the inside rim of the sunglasses (in this example, the Three of Hearts).

2 Place the force card on the bottom of the deck and you are ready to begin.

1 Perform the Hindu Force on a volunteer (see page 22). Have him remember the card, but not show anyone else. He should place the card face down on the table.

2 Pick a different volunteer (the birthday person) and slowly hand her the sunglasses. It is important that you place the glasses on her face slowly. Make sure she is the only person to see the word "Three of Hearts." You can even use your finger to lightly tap the word.

3 Ask the volunteer with the sunglasses if she can tell which card was chosen. She will most likely play along with your hint and say, "Yes, I think it is the Three of Hearts!"

4 Have the volunteer remove the chosen card and show the audience. As the audience applauds, remove the sunglasses from the volunteer and use your right thumb to secretly wipe off the writing. You can now place the sunglasses down on the table without fear of anyone working out the secret.

THEORY: VOLUNTEERS

Many magicians make use of volunteers picked from the audience to help with effects. It is important to judge which volunteers from the audience will be suitable for your tricks. There is no guaranteed formula for choosing the right volunteers, but here are a few guidelines:

Look for people who are clearly having fun and enjoying themselves.

People who choose to sit near the front are generally keen to help the magician.

Select a person who has contrasting features to you.

Women generally make good volunteers, as they are less likely to challenge the magician.

CONFETTI TO CANDY

POUR CONFETTI INTO A CUP—IT MAGICALLY TURNS INTO CANDY!

REQUIREMENTS:

2 large styrofoam cups

A sheet of cardboard

Paper plate

Glue

Scissors

Paper clips

Confetti

Some candy

PREPARATION

1 Roll the cardboard into a tube slightly taller than the styrofoam cup. Use the paper clips to secure the tube in place. Remove the bottom from one of the cups and glue a new fake bottom into it about two-thirds of the way down from the top.

2 Place this prepared cup inside the other cup and trim the rim so that is appears to look like one cup.

3 Place the candy under the fake bottom of the prepared cup. Nest both cups together and put some confetti in the top compartment.

Pull a long stick of candy out of a matchbox that is far too small to hold it!

PREPARATION:
Cut two slits in the back flap of the tray of the matchbox. Place the candy stick in the tray with the end resting through the flap in the tray. The rest of the candy rests in the left palm. You can leave some matches in the tray. Replace the tray into the box.

PERFORMANCE:
Display the matchbox and make a remark about the size of it. Open the box, reach in, and grab the end of the candy and pull it out. People will be flabbergasted at the unexpected size of the candy you remove! Close the matchbox and place it on the table.

 Pour the confetti out of the cup onto the paper plate and casually turn the cup upside down to show it is empty. Now pour the confetti back into the cup.

 Place the tube over the cup. Make a magical gesture and use the left thumb and fingers to grip the tube at the top. Remove the tube and secretly remove the prepared cup, keeping it hidden inside. Once removed, the prepared cup is held in place by the top paper clip of the tube.

3 Place the tube (with the prepared cup hidden inside) behind the table. Pour the candy out.

VANISHING CANDLE

A CANDLE INSTANTLY VANISHES AT YOUR FINGERTIPS!

REQUIREMENTS:

Elastic cord approximately 12 inches (30 cm) in length

Safety pin

Small bulldog clip

PREPARATION

1 Attach the bulldog clip to one end of the elastic cord and the safety pin to the other end.

2 Attach the safety pin on the inside of your right jacket sleeve at the top. Let the elastic cord drop down your sleeve—the bulldog clip should hang roughly 1 inch (2.5 cm) from the end of your right sleeve.

**SPOTLIGHT:
TOMMY WONDER**

Tommy Wonder (real name Jacobus Bemelman) was a Dutch magician and author of the highly praised *Books of Wonder*, a two-volume set describing original magic effects and discussions on the theory of magic. Wonder took second prize at the World Championships of Magic in 1979 and 1988.

1 When you are ready to perform, secretly reach inside your right sleeve and grip the bulldog clip between your right thumb and first finger.

2 With your left hand remove a candle from the birthday cake. Place it into your right hand as you ask a volunteer for a lighter. Carefully place the bottom of the candle into the clasp of the bulldog clip; your right hand fingers will keep the bulldog clip hidden.

TIP

Make sure the candle is completely extinguished before letting it shoot up your sleeve. As a safety precaution, you can perform the effect without lighting the candle too.

3 Retrieve the lighter and with the left hand light the candle. Put the lighter down on the table and in one swift movement, blow the candle out as the left hand approaches to apparently grab the candle. At the same time, let go of the bulldog clip and let the candle shoot up your sleeve.

4 Slowly open the left hand to show the candle has vanished in a puff of smoke!

> **MAGIC IS BELIEVING IN YOURSELF; IF YOU CAN DO THAT, YOU CAN MAKE ANYTHING HAPPEN.**
> JOHANN WOLFGANG VON GOETHE

CHAPTER 4

RESTAURANT MAGIC

THERE'S NO BETTER FEELING AS A CHILD THAN HEARING THE WORDS "WE ARE GOING OUT TO EAT."

And there is no better feeling for parents knowing they don't need to cook! Dining with the family or friends will never be the same again, for the dinner table shall become your stage.

While everyone waits for the food to arrive, you entertain them with magical marvels, such as making a toothpick vanish with your bare hands and transforming a fork into a knife!

This chapter will equip you with amazing magic effects that make use of nothing more than objects found when dining at a restaurant, but please try not to get carried away . . . nobody likes cold food!

THEORY: SLEIGHTS

Sleight of hand usually refers to magic done by manipulation with the hands and is often necessary for the magic effect to work. Sleight of hand and acting skills are two key elements of magic, and they need to work together to achieve a successful performance. Practice slowly, then build up to the real-time speed needed.

TRAVELING NAPKINS

MAKE A NAPKIN FROM YOUR DINNER TABLE VANISH AND APPEAR—IN YOUR GUESTS' HANDS!

REQUIREMENTS:

3 napkins of the same color

PERFORMANCE

PREPARATION

Secretly crumple one of the napkins into a small ball and place it in your right pants' pocket.

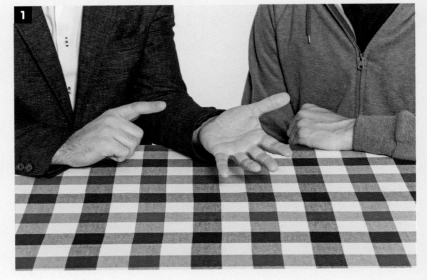

**THEORY:
MOMENT OF RELAXATION**

There are key moments in your performance that are most suitable for misdirection. When you have completed an effect and your audience has begun applauding they are less alert; if you attempt a secret move then, it is less likely to be seen.

1 Hold the crumpled napkin in your right hand and perform the French Drop (see page 30).

2 With your right hand, reach into the right pocket and remove the extra crumpled napkin to supposedly show that the napkin has traveled into your right pocket. The other napkin remains hidden in the right Finger Palm position (see page 28).

3 Instruct the volunteer to place his left hand out with the palm up. Carefully shift the napkin from Finger Palm to behind the napkin held at the right fingertips. It should appear to be just one napkin. Squeeze these napkins tightly and place them into the volunteer's open left hand. Instruct him to squeeze his hand closed tightly.

4 Pick up another napkin off the table, crumple it into a small ball, and execute the French Drop again.

5 Instruct the volunteer to open his right hand. It appears as though the napkin has magically traveled into his hand! As he reacts, secretly drop the concealed napkin in your right hand into your lap, and show your hands empty.

JUMPING SPOTS ON KNIFE

MAKE SPOTS MAGICALLY APPEAR AND VANISH ON A KNIFE!

REQUIREMENTS:

A knife

A napkin

Some water

PREPARATION

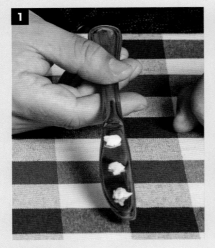

1 Tear six small pieces of paper from a napkin. Use a little bit of water to stick these paper spots onto the knife. Put three spots on each side of the knife blade.

2 There is one sleight used in this effect. Hold the knife in the right hand between the thumb and fingers with the blade facing down.

3 To display the opposite side of the knife, twist your wrist toward yourself so the knife turns over, but as your wrist turns over, use the right thumb to push the handle of the knife so the handle turns over at the same time your hand turns over. This appears to show both sides of the knife and is known as the paddle move.

4 Reverse the action, twisting your wrist back again.

PERFORMANCE

1 Display the knife in the right hand as shown.

2 Twist the right wrist to show three spots on either side of the knife blade (do not execute the paddle move).

3 Return to the starting position and remove the middle spot. Execute the paddle move and it will appear as though the middle spot vanished from the back of the knife as well.

4 Now remove the spot closest to the handle of the knife and execute the paddle move again.

5 Remove the final spot and execute the paddle move; it will appear as though the knife is blank.

6 With a quick shake of the wrist, quickly twist the knife between the right thumb and fingers to make all the spots magically reappear! Use the paddle move to show they have reappeared on both sides. Finally, out of view of your audience, remove the spots and hand out the spot-free knife for examination if you like.

TAKE IT FURTHER:
What about using different colored spots on the knife? You could try a traffic light theme.

TIPS

Try to work on individual pieces of the magic effect. Start with the sleights, familiarize yourself with the necessary props, and then form the framework of the entire effect.

Try to rehearse in small doses; you are more likely to work out the kinks in the effect by going through it in small sections.

Read the effects description, then read it again. Observe the photographs and attempt to understand what you have to accomplish.

VANISHING SUGAR

ATTEMPT TO MAKE A SUGAR PACKET VANISH . . .
INSTEAD, ONLY THE SUGAR VANISHES!

PREPARATION

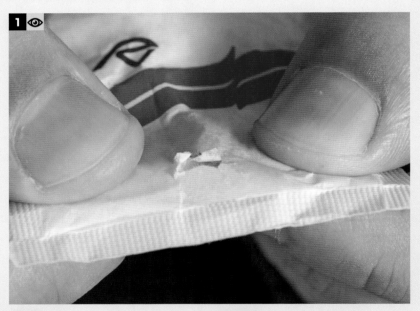

1

Tear a small slit near the end in a sugar packet; empty all of the sugar out and return the sugar packet to the table among all the other sugar packets. Do this all in secret and keep note of where the prepared sugar packet is.

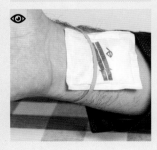

2

Place the rubber band on your right wrist. Place the full sugar packet underneath the rubber band. This should be concealed under your right sleeve.

2

**SPOTLIGHT:
CYRIL TAKAYAMA**

Cyril Takayama is an award-winning American-Japanese magician. His signature effects include pulling a real hamburger out of a menu and penetrating solid glass with his bare hand. Cyril has done multiple television specials and a large number of his videos have been uploaded to YouTube, giving him the unofficial title of magic's first cyber celebrity.

3

4

1 Look through the sugar packets on the table and casually grab the prepared sugar packet.

2 Hold the sugar packet with the right thumb and first finger. Give the packet a shake near the volunteer's ear. The sound of the sugar packet up your right sleeve will convince the volunteer that the sugar packet is still full.

3 Explain that you will attempt to make the sugar packet vanish. Place it into the left fist and make a magical gesture.

4 Open the left hand in confusion and explain that the effect has gone wrong. Dramatically tear open the sugar packet (along the tear you made earlier) and attempt to pour the sugar into the left hand. Remark that the packet has not vanished, but the sugar has!

SILVERWARE TRANSFORMATION

TRANSFORM A FORK INTO A KNIFE WITH A NAPKIN.

REQUIREMENTS:

A napkin

A knife

A fork

PERFORMANCE

1 Place the knife on the table parallel to you. Place the center of the napkin over the knife with one corner closest to you.

2 Place the fork on top of the napkin slightly behind the knife.

3 Pick up the corner of the napkin closest to you and fold it over just short of the opposite corner.

TAKE IT FURTHER:
Why only cutlery? What about turning a sealed paper straw into an opened straw?

4

5

6

6

Suck water through your ear—it comes out your mouth!

PREPARATION:
Secretly retain some water in your mouth.

PERFORMANCE:
Place a straw into a glass that is one-third filled with water. Hold the glass in your right hand and place the straw against your right ear. By tilting the glass backward it will appear as though the water is sucked up into the straw. You can now spit out the water from your mouth!

4 Carefully pick up the knife and fork through the napkin and roll the napkin around them toward you.

5 Continue to roll the napkin until the shorter corner rolls and pops out from underneath. The longer corner will be closest to you and the shorter corner furthest away. This indicates the napkin has turned over.

6 Finish by pulling the longer corner toward you and the shorter corner away from you. When the napkin unfolds completely, the knife will be on top and the fork underneath—a magical transformation!

PENETRATING CORK

COVER A CORK WITH A NAPKIN; SLAM YOUR HAND DOWN AND THE CORK PENETRATES YOUR COFFEE MUG!

REQUIREMENTS:

2 identical corks

A coffee mug

A secret accomplice

PREPARATION

1 A secret accomplice is needed for this effect. He will be the last person asked to feel the cork under the napkin, but instead of just feeling the cork, he will secretly take the cork away concealed in his hand.

2 Secretly place one of the corks underneath the coffee mug on the table.

PERFORMANCE

1 Display the cork between your right thumb and fingers. The left hand picks up the napkin and covers the cork from the top downward; the napkin is stretched around the top and sides of the cork and would hold it shape even if the cork were removed; the bottom remains open.

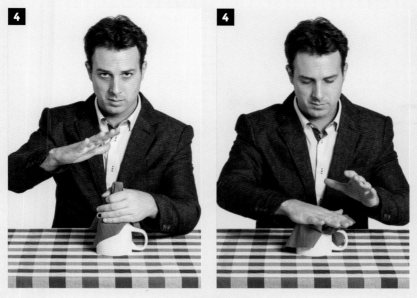

4

4

TAKE IT FURTHER

What about using other items? How about a sugar packet, sugar cube, or coffee creamer? The effect can also be accomplished without a secret accomplice—simply execute the same move from the effect "Sharpener Vanish" (see page 44); the original cork secretly falls into your lap after the final volunteer feels underneath the napkin.

5

2 You now go to several volunteers in turn and offer them each the opportunity to reach underneath the napkin to feel that the cork is still there. They should state, "Yes!" if they feel it.

3 The last person you offer is your secret accomplice; he carefully conceals the cork in his hand and adds to the deception by stating that he felt the cork underneath the napkin.

4 The napkin will retain the cork shape. Carefully place the napkin on top of the upturned coffee mug. Make a magical gesture and proceed to smash the cork through the mug.

5 You can now display the napkin empty and lift up the coffee mug to reveal the cork!

TORN AND RESTORED STRAW PAPER

TEAR UP THE PAPER STRAW COVER AND MAGICALLY RESTORE IT!

PREPARATION

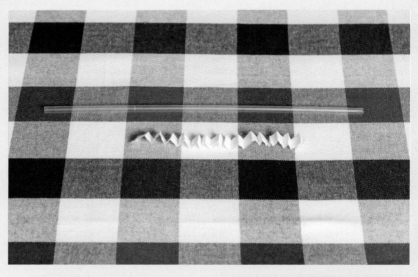

1 Carefully remove one of the paper straw covers. Concertina-fold it into a small package that can be hidden between the right thumb and first finger. Begin with this package concealed between your right thumb and fingers.

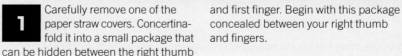

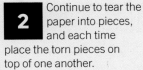
1 Remove the paper cover from a straw. Use the thumb and first fingers of each hand to tear the paper in half (keep the prepared concertina-folded package hidden between your right thumb and first finger).

2 Continue to tear the paper into pieces, and each time place the torn pieces on top of one another.

3 Now bring the fingertips of each hand together and transfer all the torn pieces between the left thumb and first finger. With the torn pieces concealed between the left thumb and first finger, open the concertina-folded package slowly. Pinch the end of the package between the tips of the left thumb and first finger and pull the fingertips gently apart.

4 It will appear as though the paper has magically restored! You can hand out the paper to a volunteer and casually drop the concealed torn pieces from between your left thumb and first finger into your pocket.

SUGAR PACKET STAB

YOU ARE ABLE TO SPEAR YOUR FINGER THROUGH A SUGAR PACKET WITH LIGHTNING SPEED!

REQUIREMENTS:

2 sugar packets

MAGIC:
IMPOSSIBLE KNOT

PREPARATION:
Tie a knot in a napkin without letting go of the ends. Ask a volunteer to try to tie a knot in a napkin without letting go of the ends—she will be unable to do so.

PERFORMANCE:
The secret is to fold your arms and pick up the napkin with one end in each hand; unfold your arms and pull tight—the knot will form!

PREPARATION

Carefully tear a hole in the center of one sugar packet and stick the first finger of the right hand through it. Conceal this prepared sugar packet in the right hand.

PERFORMANCE

1 The right hand (concealing the prepared sugar packet) rests in your lap as your left hand picks up a sugar packet off the table.

2 The left hand tosses the sugar packet into the air and catches it. On the second throw, the right hand approaches to apparently spear the sugar packet in midair. In reality, the right hand snatches the sugar packet out of the air and at the same time extends the right first finger to reveal the speared sugar packet.

3 The speared sugar packet can be removed off the right first finger and handed out to a volunteer as the right hand drops the concealed sugar packet into your lap.

PSYCHIC WAITER

A SECRETLY CHOSEN DRINK IS ORDERED OFF THE MENU. YOU SEND YOUR THOUGHTS TELEPATHICALLY TO THE WAITER, AND HE BRINGS THE CORRECT DRINK!

PREPARATION

1 Before you are seated at your table, secretly tell your waiter that when he sees you place both your hands to your head, he is to bring you an ice-cold lemonade.

2 If you stretch out your right hand toward him he is to bring you an ice-cold orange juice.

PERFORMANCE

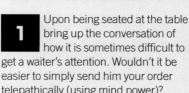

1 Upon being seated at the table bring up the conversation of how it is sometimes difficult to get a waiter's attention. Wouldn't it be easier to simply send him your order telepathically (using mind power)?

2 Explain to your friend that you can't decide between lemonade and orange juice. Get him to decide which one you should pick. Explain that you shall use telepathy to contact the waiter. Whichever drink he decides upon, make the appropriate hand signals to the waiter.

3 If he has remembered the hand signals, he will bring you the correct drink—your friend will be blown away by your telepathic powers.

TAKE IT FURTHER:
Why only drinks?

TRAVELING OLIVE

AN OLIVE MAGICALLY TRANSPORTS FROM YOUR LEFT HAND TO YOUR RIGHT HAND!

REQUIREMENTS:

2 olives

PERFORMANCE

1 Hold an olive in each hand at the fingertips. Place the olive in the left hand between your lips.

2 Execute the French Drop (see page 30) with the olive in the right hand.

3 With the right fingers, remove the olive from your lips. Pretend to throw an invisible olive into the air with the left hand.

4 Simulate "catching" the invisible olive in the right hand by rotating the right wrist palm down and gently shaking the right hand. Open the right hand to reveal two olives!

COIN THROUGH NAPKIN

A COIN MAGICALLY PENETRATES A NAPKIN.

REQUIREMENTS:

A coin

A napkin

PERFORMANCE

1

1 Display the coin at the fingertips of the right hand; put the napkin over the coin, positioning the coin in the center.

2 👁

2 Pinch a small fold of the napkin between the back of the coin and the right thumb.

3

3 The left hand now lifts the napkin up and directly back over the right arm to display the coin. The left hand releases the napkin and the right wrist turns down so both layers of the napkin fall forward over the coin (the coin is secretly outside of the napkin, held in place by the small fold obtained earlier).

4 Twist the napkin around the coin so that its shape is visible through the fabric (be careful not to expose the coin).

4 👁

5 👁

5 Reposition the left hand at the base of the coin and, using the fingers of the right hand, begin to slowly pull the coin into view. It will appear as though the coin is melting through the napkin. Remove the coin completely and hand the napkin and coin to the volunteer for examination.

VANISHING TOOTHPICK

INSTANTLY MAKE A TOOTHPICK VANISH WITH YOUR BARE HANDS!

REQUIREMENTS:	PREPARATION

A toothpick

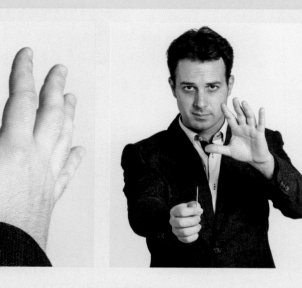

1 Wet the small area between the nail and knuckle of your right thumb.

2 Position one end of the toothpick directly on the wet area of the right thumb.

3 Bend the right thumb toward the ground and position the right first finger on the bottom of the toothpick.

 1 Display the toothpick slightly below the line of the volunteer's eyes.

2 Make a magical gesture with the left hand and simultaneously open the right hand with the palm facing the volunteer, fingers spread out; the right thumb should be straightened and the toothpick will stick to the skin.

3 It will appear as though the toothpick has vanished, as the right hand looks completely empty. To make the toothpick reappear, simply reverse the actions.

> **MAGIC IS NOT JUST FOR ENTERTAINMENT, BUT TO INSPIRE PEOPLE TO BE CREATIVE WITH THEIR LIVES.**
> AMIT KALANTRI

CHAPTER 5

OFFICE MAGIC

PUSHING PAPERS AND CRUNCHING NUMBERS, CHASING THE CLOCK UNTIL THE NEXT COFFEE BREAK—COULD THE DAY GET ANY MORE BORING?

How about showcasing your skills as a part-time forensic detective and correctly guessing when one of your colleagues is telling a lie? What about predicting a freely chosen number or surviving a dangerous game of Russian roulette with a thumbtack?!

Your office supplies will become your props as you demonstrate your devious deceptions to your colleagues. No longer will the water cooler simply provide superficial conversation and refreshment—it is your new playground of prestidigitation!

ANIMATED STICKMAN

A STICKMAN COMES TO LIFE ON YOUR STICKY NOTES AND REVEALS A SECRETLY CHOSEN CARD!

REQUIREMENTS:

A pad of sticky notes

Pencil

A deck of cards

PREPARATION

1 On the bottom sticky note use a pencil to sketch a small stickman holding the selected card next to a printer (in this example, the force card is the Two of Hearts).

2 On the second-to-last sheet, make a duplicate sketch with the stickman returning the piece of paper to the printer.

3 Continue sketching the same picture with minor changes on each consecutive page in reverse. This mimics the process used in stop animation. It is easier to sketch the animation in reverse, as you can simply trace the outline from the sheet below. The sketches should show the stickman placing a piece of paper into a printer and removing the selected card.

4 The last sheet in the notepad should be the only sheet that displays the stickman holding the selected card. The top sheet should have the title "The Amazing Rodney."

5 By riffling the right thumb off the top sheet downward, the stickman will become animated.

6 Place the force card on top of the deck.

TIP

Sketch a few different force cards on several sticky notes; these can be easily added to the notepad for repeat performances.

Read the newspaper or search online for interesting and peculiar stories that you could adapt for the context of your magic effect. Television, joke books, and listening to what your friends say could spark the creative flame for you. Examine the possibilities that the props in the magic effect present. For example, if the effect involves beads, maybe the premise for your patter could revolve around jewelry.

1 Begin by displaying the notepad and introducing the stickman, Rodney. Explain that he has a special talent—he can read minds!

2 Pick up the deck of cards and execute the Slip Force (see page 26) on your colleague. Have her place the selected card face down on the table.

3 With your left hand, pick up the notepad and use the right thumb to riffle down the edges of the sheets. Begin with the top sheet and slowly work the right thumb down. The riffling action will animate the stickman printing the selected card!

4 When the final sticky note sheet is reached, peel it off and hand it to your colleague as a souvenir!

ACROBATIC LINKING PAPER CLIPS

WITH A MAGICAL GESTURE YOU LINK TWO PAPER CLIPS IN MIDAIR!

REQUIREMENTS:

2 paper clips

A dollar bill

PERFORMANCE

1 Fold the dollar bill with one-third underneath itself.

2 Attach a paper clip on the edge as shown.

3 Fold the other end of the bill in the opposite direction to the first fold. Attach the second paper clip on the edge of the top fold made earlier. The result is a "Z" fold in the dollar bill.

4 Carefully hold the bill at each end and swiftly pull it apart—the two paper clips will link themselves together as they fly through the air!

LIE FOR ME

ACCURATELY DETECT WHEN YOUR COLLEAGUE IS TELLING A LIE!

REQUIREMENTS:

A sheet of paper

A permanent marker

PERFORMANCE

1 Tear a strip off the bottom of the sheet of paper. Hand the permanent marker to your colleague and explain to her that while your back is turned, she is to write in the middle of the sheet of paper one fact about herself that no one knows.

2 Once she has completed this, instruct your colleague to tear off a piece from each end so that she has three pieces roughly the same size.

3 One piece has a fact that is true. Instruct her to write one fact that is not true about herself on each of the other two pieces.

4 Have your colleague mix up the pieces of paper and turn them face up on the table in a row. Explain that you can detect lies and ask your colleague the same question three times in a row: "Is this fact true?" Instruct her to answer each time with, "No, this fact is not true."

5 Follow the procedure three times and then dramatically reveal which fact she was lying about. You are able to do this because during the tearing procedure two strips will be uneven on only one side, while the center strip will be uneven on two sides.

PEN THROUGH DOLLAR BILL

YOU BORROW A COLLEAGUE'S DOLLAR BILL AND PUSH YOUR PEN RIGHT THROUGH IT—THE BILL REMAINS UNHARMED!

TIP

By tearing the envelope in half along the slit made earlier, you can destroy the evidence after the effect and leave the envelope for examination.

PREPARATION

1 Carefully cut a slit across the back of the envelope, and directly below the slit, cut a small cross through both the front and the back of the envelope. The envelope should be slightly larger than a dollar bill. (If you struggle to find the correct size envelope, simply trim an existing one.)

1 Hold the envelope with the slit facing toward you. Borrow a colleague's dollar bill and slide the bill into the envelope, making sure the bottom end of the bill comes out of the slit at the back.

2 Now secretly fold the bill upward using your left thumb. Pinch the bill against the top of the envelope with your left thumb and fingers.

3 Pick up the pen with your right hand and push it through the cross, starting at the side facing you. It will look as though the pen is penetrating the dollar bill!

4 Remove the pen, and release the bill from beneath the left thumb. Quickly pull the bill out of the envelope with the right hand—it is unharmed!

CARD ON FAN

A SECRETLY CHOSEN CARD APPEARS STUCK TO YOUR COLLEAGUE'S FAN!

PREPARATION

1 Secretly attach the duplicate force card (in this example, the Three of Hearts) to one of the blades of a fan. When the fan is operational, the spinning blades will make the card undetectable.

2 Construct the gimmicked card from the effect "Card in Balloon" (see page 62). Place this gimmicked card in the center of the deck.

1 Hold the deck of cards in your left hand and use the right first and second fingers to riffle (see page 20) up the edge of the deck. Starting at the bottom, begin slowly riffling and ask your colleague to call, "Stop!" Time your riffle carefully and the cards will automatically stop at the prepared double card. Ask your colleague to remember this card.

2 You will now spring the cards from your right hand by bending them as shown. The deck is held with the right thumb on the bottom end of the deck and the right fingers on the top end. Aim the cards toward the fan.

TIP

When gathering the cards up off the table, make sure you pick up the gimmicked card; this will keep your colleague from discovering the secret.

3 Spring the cards at the spinning blades of the fan. Once all the cards have fallen on the table and floor, ask your colleague whether she can spot her card.

4 Gather all the cards up one by one; she will be unable to find her card. Suggest switching the fan off. Once the blades stop spinning your colleague will be presented with a truly remarkable sight—her chosen card stuck to one of the blades!

WHAT IS IN MY HAND?

YOUR COLLEAGUE IS ABLE TO CORRECTLY GUESS WHAT IS HIDDEN IN YOUR HAND—AND HE'LL HAVE NO CLUE HOW!

REQUIREMENTS:

Several sheets of paper

Pencil

4 quarters ($1.00) in loose change

PREPARATION

1 Print the list of items below on several pieces of paper.

2 Hold the four quarters concealed in your right fist. Try to pick a volunteer whom you do not know.

1. Dice	11. Sock	21. Toothpick	31. Marble	41. Shell	51. Salt	61. Biscuit
2. Match	12. Card	22. LEGO brick	32. Popcorn	42. Block	52. Rock	62. Staple
3. Pin	13. Photo	23. Keys	33. Nail	43. Frog	53. Tape	63. Four quarters
4. Egg	14. Sticker	24. Rice	34. Flower	44. Wrist watch	54. Buck	64. Sugar cube
5. Nothing	15. Lid	25. Guitar pick	35. Twig	45. Dollar	55. Pen cap	65. Inkblot
6. Yo-yo	16. Paper clip	26. Shoelace	36. Spare change	46. Earrings	56. Battery	66. Pill
7. Chip	17. Magnet	27. Coins	37. Rubber band	47. Pea	57. Badge	67. Paper
8. Eraser	18. $1.00	28. Post-it	38. Flash drive	48. Bouncing ball	58. Tweezers	68. Plastic
9. Money	19. Toy car	29. Buttons	39. Dirt	49. Leaf	59. String	69. Crayon
10. Foil	20. Tooth	30. Plug	40. Thimble	50. Grape	60. Insect	70. Pin

1 Casually show the lists to the volunteer and explain that one of those items is concealed in your right fist. It will be his job to work out which one.

2 Ask the volunteer to think of his age and to add the two digits together; for example, 23 = 2 + 3 = 5. Now instruct him to subtract this number (5) from his age and remember the total. For example, 23 – 5 = 18.

3 Ask the volunteer to go through the lists and find the item that is next to his new number. In this example: 18 = $1.00. Have him announce this randomly chosen item, and dramatically open your fist to reveal exactly one dollar!

MAGIC: A READING TEST

> **PLEASE GIVE ME A A CHANCE**
>
> **LONDON IN THE THE WINTER**
>
> **MAN IN THE THE MOON**

You casually flash three basic sentences to a colleague—chances are, she misses all three mistakes!

PREPARATION:
Construct three signs on index cards as shown in the photo. (Man in the the moon; Please give me a a chance; London in the the the winter.)

PERFORMANCE:
Display the signs one at a time to your colleague and instruct her to read each one aloud. Chances are she will not pick up the repetitions in each sentence.

STATIONERY PREDICTION

YOUR COLLEAGUE WILL THINK YOU HAVE PSYCHIC POWERS WHEN YOU CORRECTLY PREDICT WHICH ITEM SHE WILL CHOOSE!

REQUIREMENTS:

2 sheets of cardstock

Scissors

Paper

Envelope

Stapler

Eraser

Glue stick

Calculator

PREPARATION

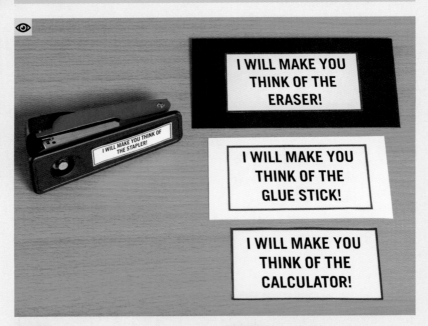

I WILL MAKE YOU THINK OF THE ERASER!

I WILL MAKE YOU THINK OF THE GLUE STICK!

I WILL MAKE YOU THINK OF THE CALCULATOR!

I WILL MAKE YOU THINK OF THE STAPLER!

1 Cut two sheets of cardstock that will fit inside the envelope. On the front of one cardstock, print, "Point to an item." On the reverse side of this card, print, "I will make you think of the glue stick!" On the other card, print, "I will make you think of the calculator!"

2 Place both these cards into the envelope with the "Point to an item" card closest to the flap. On the front of the envelope print, "I will make you think of the eraser!" On the bottom of the stapler stick a small piece of paper with the words "I will make you think of the stapler!" printed on it.

Find out your volunteers' names and use them. Look them in the eye when using their names and they will look you in the face and not down at your hands.

By getting your volunteers actively involved in the magic effects, other spectators will watch them and not you.

POINT TO
AN ITEM

1 Carefully take the "Point to an item" card out of the envelope and lay it on the table. Place the glue stick, eraser, stapler, and calculator opposite the corners of the card (be careful not to let your colleague see underneath the stapler). Make sure you leave the envelope on the table in view.

2 Explain that you will magically send her the thought of one of the items. She must try to "pick up" your thought.

3 Instruct your colleague to announce the thought she "received." The effect can now end in several different ways, depending on which item she names:

A. If she names the glue stick, turn the "Point to an item" card around to reveal your message, "I will make you think of the glue stick!"

B. If she names the eraser, turn over the envelope to reveal your message, "I will make you think of the eraser!"

C. If she names the calculator, open the envelope and slide out the card with your message, "I will make you think of the calculator!"

D. If she names the stapler, get her to turn the stapler over and read your message, "I will make you think of the stapler!" You can then make a joke and ask her to turn over the remaining items—to her shock, she will find nothing under the other items!

RUSSIAN ROULETTE

YOUR VOLUNTEER SELECTS WHICH PAPER CONES YOU SHOULD CRUSH WITH YOUR FINGER—THE REMAINING CONE CONTAINS A THUMBTACK!

REQUIREMENTS:

2 sticky notes

Thumbtack

Pencil

Scissors

Glue

PREPARATION

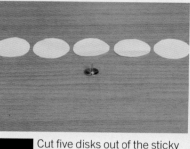

1 Cut five disks out of the sticky notes, each with a diameter of roughly 2 inches (5 cm).

2 Stack the five disks on top of one another and cut a triangle out of the disks by making two cuts at 90 degrees to the center of the disks. Remove these triangles.

3 Apply glue to the edge of one side of the disk and glue into a cone shape. Do this for all five disks to make five small cone shapes.

4 Make a small cut in the base of one of the cones. This will be a secret mark for you to identify this cone.

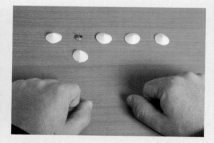

5 Place the five cones in a row on the table and place the thumbtack underneath the marked cone. In this example the marked cone is second from your left, with the mark closest to you.

1 Explain to your colleague that you are going to play a fun game of elimination.

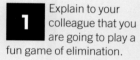

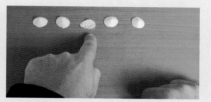

2 Begin by pointing to any two cones (but do not point to the marked cone); ask your colleague which cone should be eliminated. Whichever one he decides upon, use your right first finger to crush the cone flat.

3 Now instruct your colleague to point to any two cones. He might point to the marked cone; if he does, simply eliminate the other cone he pointed to. Do so by crushing it with the right first finger.

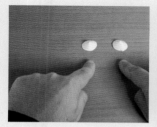

4 It is now your turn to point to two cones. Never point to the marked cone; this way, your colleague can never eliminate it. Whichever cone he decides upon, crush it with the right first finger. Continue until two cones are left.

5 There are now two cones left on the table (one is the marked cone). Explain to your colleague that you will do the last round differently; instruct him to point to one of the cones. If he points to the cone without the mark, use the right thumb to crush the cone. If he points to the marked cone, explain that you will keep that one aside and crush the other one. Either way, the situation will be interpreted as being different and thus not arouse suspicion.

6 All that remains is to dramatically lift the final cone and reveal the thumbtack! Your colleague will be shocked to find out that the "fun game" has actually been a game of Russian roulette!

WARNING:

Even though the process for this effect is safe, there is a still a risk of injury. Please be careful when performing this effect. Make double sure you have set up the effect properly and that you keep track of the marked cone at all times.

WHEN IT GOES WRONG: If a volunteer ruins your magic effect, simply stop and move on to the next effect as quickly as possible. Try not to blame him or make him feel bad.

RISING RING ON RUBBER BAND

YOUR COLLEAGUE'S RING DEFIES GRAVITY BY SLIDING UP A RUBBER BAND!

PREPARATION

1 Break the rubber band. Hold the ring between the left thumb and fingertips; insert roughly ¾ inch (2 cm) of the top of the rubber band through the ring.

2 Pinch the band and the ring between the left thumb and first finger with the back of the hand facing your colleague. With the right-hand thumb and first finger, pinch the band directly under the ring and pull the band taut.

3 Let the ring slide down the band and rest gently on the right first finger. From the audience's perspective, it appears as though you are simply holding the band between your hands.

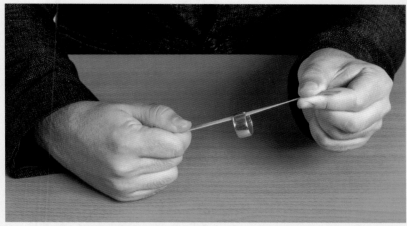

1 Begin by holding your left hand slightly higher than your right hand at an angle of roughly 45 degrees. Slowly release pressure from the right thumb and first finger—the ring will remain in contact with the band and as the band slowly retracts it will appear as though the ring is rising up the band.

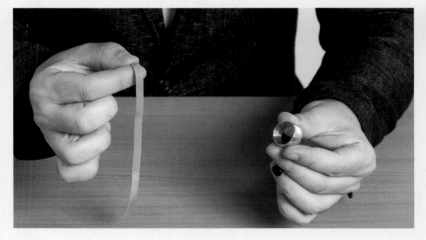

2 Allow the band to retract all the way until the ring reaches your left hand. The left fingers remove the ring by sliding it off the band— this helps sell the illusion. You can now hand back the ring and offer the rubber band for examination.

MAGICAL NUMBER PREDICTION

PREDICT THE RESULT OF FREELY CHOSEN NUMBERS THAT APPEAR ON YOUR CALENDAR!

REQUIREMENTS:

A pencil

Paper

A calendar

PREPARATION

On the current day on the calendar, write in bold, "I predict you will choose the number 34!"

PERFORMANCE

1 Write the numbers 1 through 16 on the paper in 4 by 4 grid formation.

2 Ask your colleague to name a number from 1 to 16. Circle the chosen number and then draw two lines through the corresponding row and column.

Your tie magically penetrates through your neck!

PREPARATION:
Knot the tie without putting it around your neck. Carefully fold the loop in half and tuck these two flaps under your collar. The tie will appear normal from the front.

PERFORMANCE:
Explain to your colleague that it is a rather hot day and tug hard on your tie—it will appear as though the tie has penetrated your neck!

3 Ask him to choose another number that does not have a line through it. Circle this number and draw two lines through the corresponding row and column as you did previously.

4 Repeat the same process until there is one number left that has not been crossed out. Ask your colleague to add this number to the numbers he has already chosen. In this example it is 3 + 5 + 12 + 14 = 34.

5 Direct his attention to the current day on the calendar— he will be amazed to see you correctly predicted the number 34!

> **THAT'S THE THING ABOUT MAGIC; YOU'VE GOT TO KNOW IT'S STILL HERE, ALL AROUND US, OR IT JUST STAYS INVISIBLE FOR YOU.**
> CHARLES DE LINT

CHAPTER 6

MAGIC AT THE BAR

THE BAR PEANUTS HAVE DRIED UP AND SO HAS THE CONVERSATION—IT'S TIME FOR YOU TO DISPLAY YOUR NEWLY HONED SKILLS OF WIZARDRY. A QUIET DRINK WITH FRIENDS ON A FRIDAY NIGHT WILL NOW BE THE TALKING POINT OF THE WEEKEND.

Instantly freeze a beer with the power of your mind; make a coin magically penetrate a beer coaster; or relight a burnt match! These are just some of the effects that will keep the bar flowing with wonder.

The next round is on you, but I hope the bartender is ready for money that will be plucked from thin air!

INEXHAUSTIBLE MATCH

YOU DISPLAY YOUR MAGICAL POWERS BY RELIGHTING A BURNT MATCH!

REQUIREMENTS:

A box of matches

Black permanent marker

TIPS ON TALKING

Speech plays a vital role in connecting with your audience:

1. Clarity: Good articulation will ensure crisp, clear communication.

2. Volume: You may have to increase your volume so that everyone can hear you.

3. Pitch: Avoid a pitch that is too high or too low. Strive for a natural pitch that is pleasing and mellow.

4. Tempo: Don't speak too quickly. On the other hand, a slow speaker may bore the audience.

5. Variety: Avoid a monotonous voice. Train your voice to be varied, musical, pleasant, and friendly.

PREPARATION

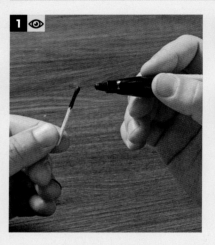

1 Color the head and a small section of the wood of one match using the black permanent marker.

2 Carry this prepared match in your pocket or in the box of matches. Secretly drop it into an ashtray when no one is looking.

PERFORMANCE

1 Grab a genuinely burnt match from an ashtray and make a remark about the possibility of lighting a burnt match. Your attempt will be unsuccessful, but offer to try one more time.

2 This time, grab the prepared match and strike it—it will ignite to the amazement of the audience!

FREEZE!

INSTANTLY FREEZE A BEER BY SIMPLY TAPPING IT AGAINST A TABLE.

REQUIREMENTS:
A few glass bottles of beer
A freezer

PREPARATION

Place a few of these beers in the freezer until they are almost frozen. The beers should not be solid or slushy; they should be very cold but still liquid.

PERFORMANCE

1 Take the bottle out of the freezer and rest it on a solid surface like concrete or stone.

2 Grip the bottle firmly with the left hand around the neck and hold it several inches above the solid surface.

3 Strike the bottle against the solid surface firmly with one movement (not breaking the glass). It is better to hit it too softly than to break the glass.

TIP

If you experience problems getting the beer to freeze, chances are the liquid is not cold enough. Place it back in the freezer and try a little later. This effect will work with most carbonated drinks.

4 If done correctly, the liquid will slowly begin to freeze by the bubbles created from the strike. This usually takes five to ten seconds.

VANISHING MATCHES

MAKE THE MATCHES IN A MATCHBOX VANISH!

TIP

This effect is perfect for a couple or for two people who are related, such as siblings or cousins.

PREPARATION

1 Half fill a matchbox with matches and place this box under a rubber band on your right forearm. This matchbox will be hidden under your sleeve.

PERFORMANCE

Two forks are balanced on the tip of a match on top of your friend's beer bottle!

PERFORMANCE:

Step 1: Interlock the prongs of two forks together. Insert a match between the prongs in the middle.

Step 2: Balance the non-striking end of the match on the rim of a bottle. This might take some careful adjusting until the center of balance is found.

Step 3: Let go of the match and forks and invite the audience to marvel at the unusual spectacle.

1 Carefully pick up the empty matchbox in your right hand and shake it. The sound of the rattling matches will come from the hidden matchbox up your sleeve. Ask the volunteer to try and guess how many matches are in the box.

2 Once she has given you her guess, wave your hand over the box in a magical gesture.

3 Open the matchbox and show that the matches have disappeared! You can even hand the matchbox to the volunteer to inspect.

KEEP THE CHANGE

YOU CORRECTLY PREDICT A SELECTED CARD AND LEAVE YOUR VOLUNTEER WITH A TIP HE'LL NEVER FORGET.

REQUIREMENTS:

A deck of cards

2 quarters

PREPARATION

1 Place any Two and Five on top of the deck (the suits do not matter, just the values) with the deck facedown; the top card is a Two followed by a Five.

2 Place the two quarters inside the card case with the deck of cards. Close the card case and lay the case on the table.

1 Carefully remove the deck of cards from the case (be careful not to let the quarters be seen or heard). Spread the deck between your hands and pull out any Three (the suit does not matter). Place this card in the card case without showing the audience and state that it is your prediction.

2 Turn to the first volunteer and execute the Slip Force (see page 26). Turn to the second volunteer and execute the Slip Force.

3 Have the volunteers display their selected cards to each other. Instruct them to add the values of the two selections together without telling anyone. A Jack would represent 11, a Queen 12, a King 13, and an Ace 1. Once they have completed this, instruct them to divide their answer by two.

4 Have the volunteers announce their final answer aloud. Look slightly puzzled when they remark, "Three and a half!" Carefully remove the prediction card (Three) from the card case. Stall a bit, then tip the card case and let the two quarters slide out . . . "and a half!"

MAGIC: SUSPENDED GLASS

Challenge your friends to balance a glass on a dollar bill between two other glasses.

REQUIREMENTS:
A crisp dollar bill and 3 glasses of the same size

PERFORMANCE:
Step 1: Concertina-fold the dollar bill horizontally, making as many small folds as possible.

Step 2: Place the dollar bill between the two glasses and rest the third glass upside down on top of the bill. The creases will have made the bill strong enough to support the weight of the glass.

PENETRATING COIN THROUGH COASTER

A COIN PENETRATES A BEER COASTER!

REQUIREMENTS:

A glass tumbler

Coaster

2 coins

PREPARATION

1 Hold the coin on the fingertips of the right hand and cover the coin with the coaster. Place the other coin in view on the table.

MAGIC: ON TAP!

Tap a matchbox and make a coin rise to the top without touching it!

REQUIREMENTS:
A matchbox and a coin.

PERFORMANCE:
Step 1: Hold the matchbox by the left long edge between the left thumb and fingers. The inner tray should face away from you.

Step 2: Place the coin inside the bottom edge of the back of the matchbox cover so half of the coin is exposed.

Step 3: Use the right first finger to repeatedly tap the top right corner of the matchbox. The coin will slowly creep up into the matchbox and after several taps, emerge from the top of the matchbox!

1 You will now display both sides of the coaster while concealing the coin in the right hand. As the right hand turns over, the right fingers turn in with the coin sliding underneath; the right hand turns back, reversing the actions.

2 Carefully place the coaster on top of the glass, secretly trapping the coin between the rim of the glass and the coaster.

3 Pick up the coin on the table and execute the French Drop (see page 30).

4 The left hand now pretends to push the coin through the coaster; at the same time, the right first finger nudges the coaster, dislodging the concealed coin.

5 As soon as the concealed coin contacts the bottom of the glass, lift the coaster off the glass with the right hand.

6 Tip the coin out of the glass with the left hand and place the coaster on the table, hiding the left hand's concealed coin underneath.

APPEARING CIGARETTE

PRODUCE A CIGARETTE FROM THIN AIR!

PREPARATION

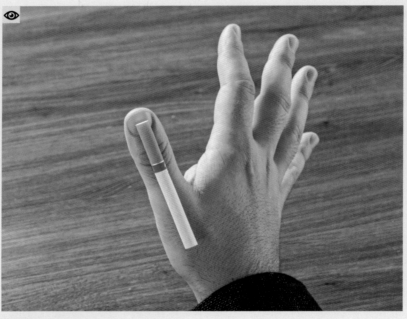

1 Wet the small area between the nail and knuckle of the right thumb (saliva will work). Place the end of the cigarette with the filter against the wet area on the right thumb.

1 Display both hands with the palms directly facing the volunteer. All the fingers are pointed directly parallel to the volunteer's eyes. Be sure to keep the cigarette concealed behind the right thumb.

2 Both hands appear to be empty as the fingers are spread open. In one swift motion, move the right hand forward and bend the right thumb in behind the right first finger. This will seem to make the cigarette appear out of thin air.

3 Immediately hand the cigarette to the volunteer to examine. While he examines the cigarette you have plenty of time to secretly place another cigarette behind your right thumb in preparation to repeat the effect another time.

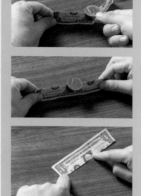

An impossible effect in which a coin balances on the edge of a dollar bill.

REQUIREMENTS:
A large coin and a crisp dollar bill

PERFORMANCE:
Step 1: Fold a crisp dollar bill in half along its long edge. Fold the bill in half again, this time along its width.

Step 2: Place the bill on the table with the folded edge closest to you. Carefully place the coin on the central folded "V" shape. Using both hands, carefully pinch the bill between the thumb and fingers. Gently pull the edges of the bill away from each other. The coin will magically align itself and balance in an impossible manner!

THE TRAVELING KINGS

THREE KINGS VANISH FROM WINEGLASSES ONLY TO REAPPEAR INSIDE AN ENVELOPE!

REQUIREMENTS:

A deck of cards

4 glasses

An envelope

PREPARATION

1 Place the four Kings from the deck into separate glass tumblers. Behind the King of Clubs secretly hide any three spot cards (numbered cards, not the Ace or picture cards).

2 On top of the face down deck have any twelve spot cards. Place the envelope on the table.

1 Carefully remove the King of Clubs with the three hidden spot cards behind it. It should appear to be one card. Remove another King and place it face up on the King of Clubs. Continue to remove the other two Kings, each time placing them face up on the others.

2 The left hand now holds seven faceup cards: four Kings at the front and three spot cards at the back. Turn the packet facedown and from the top place one card into each glass—these cards should have their backs facing the audience. (The three hidden spot cards go into the first three glasses, while the last four cards—the four Kings—are held as one and placed into the final glass.)

3 Remove twelve spot cards from the top of the tabled deck of cards. Place three cards into each glass in front of the cards already there.

4 Turn the glass with the Kings around so the audience can see the face of the first one. Pick up the envelope and show that it is empty. Carefully remove the Kings along with all six cards that are behind it (make it appear as one card). Place these cards into the envelope and ask a volunteer to hold it.

5 Make a magical gesture and state that all the other Kings have decided to join the traveling King! Remove the other packets of cards from the glasses one by one, showing that the Kings have vanished!

6 Take the envelope back from the volunteer and remove the four Kings one by one, dropping them back into their separate glasses. Place the envelope in your pocket to get rid of the evidence (no one will suspect that there are three extra cards left inside).

THE WORLD OF MAGIC!

YOU MIGHT FIND YOURSELF ONLY PICKING UP THIS BOOK ONCE IN A WHILE, PERFORMING FOR A FEW PEOPLE AND THEN CARRYING ON WITH YOUR LIFE.

However, be warned—the magic bug bites! It bit me years ago and I have never recovered. Luckily, the effects are positive, with continuous symptoms of wonder and astonishment. If it happens to you, you might want to find support and encouragement from fellow magicians.

Fortunately, magicians are (for the most part) quite social creatures and there are various institutions and organizations that will help you take your magic to the next level. Listed here are the three main institutions for promoting and advancing the art of magic.

THE MAGIC CIRCLE

The Magic Circle is widely considered one of the most famous magic societies in the world. It is a British organization and was founded in 1905 by a group of twenty-three amateur and professional magicians. David Devant became the first president of the Magic Circle in 1906, and its Latin motto is *"Indocilis Privata Loqui,"* which loosely translates to "not apt to disclose secrets."

Early meetings of the Magic Circle took place at St George's Hall in Langham Place; this is where David Devant and John Nevil Maskelyne were regular performers. In 1998, the Magic Circle moved to central London near Euston Station in Camden. The headquarters house a club room, theater, library, and museum.

The Magic Castle is a performance venue for professional magicians from around the world. Guests who attend an evening at the Magic Castle experience several different performances in various theaters. Entry is only allowed to members and their guests.

The Academy of Magical Arts has more than 5,000 members worldwide. To become a member you must audition before the Academy's reviewing committee. Even nonmembers can enroll in their six-week magic classes that are taught by legends in the field. Find out more at www.magiccastle.com.

THE COLLEGE OF MAGIC

The College of Magic is the only organization of its kind in the world. Located in Cape Town, South Africa, it offers a diploma program in the magical arts for adults and courses for middle school and high school students. It currently houses more than 170 young students experiencing the life-changing benefits of magic.

Founded by the current director, David Gore, the College of Magic opened its doors in 1980, providing much-needed training for aspiring performance artists and entertainers from all communities. The College of Magic's very own Magical Arts Centre was opened in 1995 and serves as the heart of magic for the Southern Hemisphere. The college is a nonprofit organization with a volunteer staff of more than forty. The organization has produced several award-winning South African performers and continues to bring magic into the lives of thousands of people each year. Find out more at www.collegeofmagic.com.

f you wish to join the Magic Circle, you must undergo a process that involves a performance exam held in front of a panel of judges. There are approximately 1,500 members; many are famous performers, including Dynamo and David Copperfield. Find out more at www.themagicccircle.co.uk.

THE MAGIC CASTLE

Located in Hollywood, California, the Magic Castle is a stunning château-esque mansion that is a nightclub for magicians and magic enthusiasts. It is also the headquarters for the Academy of Magical Arts, a nonprofit corporation aimed at promoting and developing the art of magic. The Magic Castle opened its doors in 1963 under the establishment of William Larsen Sr. and bills itself as "the most unusual private club in the world." It boasts several theaters and bars, a restaurant, and a library for members.

> **WHETHER YOU'RE SHUFFLING A DECK OF CARDS OR HOLDING YOUR BREATH, MAGIC IS PRETTY SIMPLE: IT COMES DOWN TO TRAINING, PRACTICE, AND EXPERIMENTATION, FOLLOWED UP BY RIDICULOUS PURSUIT AND RELENTLESS PERSEVERANCE.**
> DAVID BLAINE

CHAPTER 7

STREET MAGIC

A DARK ALLEYWAY, THE SMELL OF ASPHALT, SHADOWS ON A BRICK WALL ACCOMPANIED BY THE SOUND OF PASSING CARS AND PEDESTRIANS—THE STREET IS WHERE YOU BRING YOUR MAGIC TODAY. WHETHER PEOPLE ARE SITTING ON A BENCH WAITING FOR A BUS OR STANDING IN LINE FOR A HOT DOG, THEY ARE ABOUT TO EXPERIENCE ASTONISHMENT!

No need for flashy lights or smoke machines—the magic effects in this chapter are designed to be performed on the sidewalk, outside a coffee shop, in the park, or just about anywhere. Street magic is about bringing magic to the people.

Street magic is sometimes seen as a darker, more bizarre form of magic, so I hope your audience is ready to witness you levitate off the ground, turn old receipts into money, and even stop your own pulse!

THEORY: TIME LAPSE

The human memory is particularly bad at remembering specific details, especially if a lot is going on. Use this to your advantage by getting rid of your secret props on the "offbeat," or wait a while before getting rid of them.

ASHES ON ARM

THIS IS A SPOOKY EFFECT IN WHICH THE NAME OF A SECRETLY SELECTED CARD APPEARS IN ASHES ON YOUR ARM!

REQUIREMENTS:

A deck of cards

Lip balm

Pencil

Piece of paper

An ashtray

Box of matches

PREPARATION

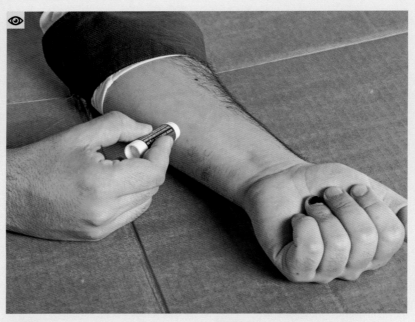

1 Place the force card on the bottom of the deck of cards (in this example it is the Seven of Diamonds).

2 Write the number "7" and the outline of a diamond shape on your left forearm with lip balm. This writing will remain invisible until the ashes are rubbed on your arm and adhere to it. This preparation is all done in secret; you are now ready to start your performance.

1 Begin with the deck of cards face down on the table. Execute the Criss-Cross Force (see page 24). Ask a volunteer to remember her selected card and to write down the name of the card on the piece of paper. She is to fold the paper into quarters with the writing on the inside.

2 Light the match and burn the paper in the ashtray (please be careful with fire). Let the paper burn completely and wait a few seconds for the ashes to cool.

SPOTLIGHT: DAVID BLAINE

Born in 1973, David Blaine is an American magician and endurance artist. He rose to fame with his various television specials and popularized the genre of magic known as "street magic." Blaine holds several world records and each year he performs across the globe for various charities. A notable performance was when he appeared on *The Oprah Winfrey Show* in 2008 and held his breath under water for 17 minutes 4½ seconds.

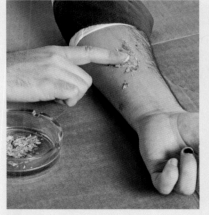

3 Pick up some of the ashes with your right hand and rub them on your left forearm. The ashes will adhere to the area you coated with lip balm, and the number and suit of the selected card will appear as if by magic!

RECEIPT TO MONEY

IN A FLASH YOUR OLD RECEIPT TURNS INTO REAL MONEY!

PREPARATION

1 Cut the receipt the exact size of the dollar bill, approximately 6 by 2½ inches (15.4 by 6.4 cm). Fold the receipt in half down the middle; unfold it and turn it over. Now fold each side in half again.

2 Concertina-fold the receipt along the creases so the end of the receipt faces your right. Put one final fold in the receipt by folding it up and toward you.

3 Unfold the receipt and repeat the exact same fold with the dollar bill.

4 Apply a small dab of rubber cement to the back of the dollar bill.

5 Attach the dollar bill to the lower right corner of the horizontal receipt. Align all the edges perfectly.

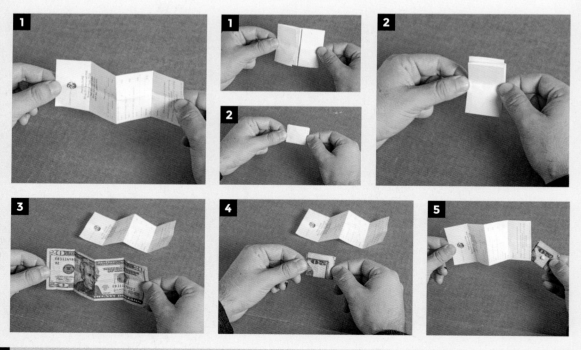

1 Hold the receipt in both hands with your fingers at the front and thumbs behind. The folded dollar bill is hidden behind the right fingers. The receipt can be displayed front and back by rotating both wrists (the folded dollar bill remains concealed behind the right fingers).

2 With the front of the receipt facing up, concertina-fold it from left to right along the creases and then fold it back toward you. The left hand aids the folding, while the right hand remains motionless.

3 Bring the right hand up to your mouth as you blow on the right hand (in the same motion, turn the folded package over).

4 As the right hand is brought down from your mouth, the right thumb pushes open the first fold of the dollar bill.

5 The left fingers immediately pinch the edge of the dollar bill and open it completely. The folded receipt is hidden behind the right fingers. The dollar bill can be displayed by rotating the wrists with the same movement from step 1.

6 Using the right thumb, the folded receipt can be pulled off and into the right Finger Palm position (see page 28). The dollar bill can now be handed out for examination while the right hand falls to the side of the body and on the offbeat pockets the folded receipt.

TIP

Try and find a receipt with the same value as the dollar bill— you can then make a remark about how a magician would get his money back!

SELF-LEVITATION

LEVITATE A FEW INCHES OFF THE GROUND IN THE STREET WITHOUT WINGS, STRINGS, OR MAGNETS!

PREPARATION

 1 Make sure that you are only performing for a small group of people. These people will need to be positioned directly behind you; any people positioned on the sides will be able to see how the effect is achieved.

2 Position yourself 6 to 8 feet (1.8 to 2.5 m) away from your audience.

PERFORMANCE

1 Turn your back to the audience and then turn about 45 degrees toward the foot you will lift off the ground.

2 Position both arms straight out from your sides and crouch somewhat.

3

4

THEORY: PEOPLE PROBLEMS

Manage your volunteers properly by giving them clear instructions, positioning them correctly, and asking questions that do not embarrass them.

Give clear, simple instructions.

If possible, give the instructions one at a time.

Check each time that they are understood.

Repeat the instructions if necessary.

 3 Press down with the toes of the right foot, allowing the left foot to be elevated off the ground.

4 The left foot that is lifted off the ground remains in the same position it would be if it were still flat on the ground.

5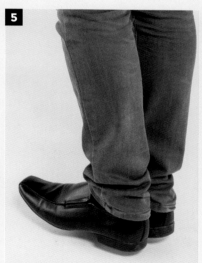

5 It will appear as though you are levitating off the ground because the audience will see your entire left foot off the ground and the right heel creates the illusion that the right foot is off the ground, too.

6 Dramatically lower the right toes and simultaneously lower your arms to your sides. Bend the knees slightly as you land to help sell the illusion of height.

TIP

Be sure to experiment with the correct angles needed to make this illusion effective. Try to levitate for only a moment, and then return to the ground.

CARD ON WINDOW

A SECRETLY SELECTED CARD MAGICALLY PENETRATES A NEARBY GLASS WINDOW!

REQUIREMENTS:

A deck of cards

Duplicate force card

Tape

Double card gimmick (see page 62)

PREPARATION

1 Take the duplicate force card (in this example it is the Three of Hearts) and secretly stick it to the outside of a window that has a curtain or blind in front of it. Use a small piece of tape and stick the duplicate force card with its face outward. Close the curtain to hide the card from view.

2 Place the double card gimmick in the center of the deck.

1 Hold the deck of cards in your left hand and use the right first and second fingers to riffle (see page 20) up the edge of the deck. Starting at the bottom, begin slowly riffling and ask the volunteer to call, "Stop!" Time your riffle carefully and the cards will automatically stop at the prepared double card. Ask the volunteer to remember this card.

2 Walk over to the window and with the left hand pull the curtain to the side while the right hand (which holds the deck) quickly puts the deck directly over the card that is outside the window. Use your back to help conceal this entire movement.

3 Have the volunteer make a magical tap against the deck and then ask the volunteer to name aloud his selection. Move the deck away from the window to reveal the one face down card stuck to the outside of the window. Dramatically drop the cards one by one, showing the faces as they fall to the floor—the Three of Hearts will not be present.

4 Have the volunteer open the window and reach outside to remove the card—he will be shocked to find that it is his selected card!

COIN THROUGH HOLE

A BORROWED COIN VISIBLY PENETRATES THROUGH A HOLE THAT IS CLEARLY TOO SMALL FOR IT TO PASS THROUGH!

REQUIREMENTS:

A playing card

Coin

Pencil

Scissors

Craft knife

PREPARATION

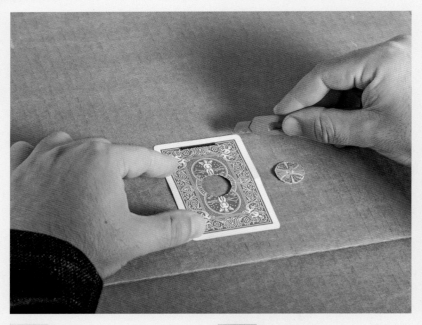

1 Fold the card in half so the faces are together. Unfold the card and use the pencil to trace a circle (slightly smaller than the coin you will use) on the face of the card at the center.

2 Use the scissors to carefully cut out this pencil circle.

3 Along the center of the top edge of the back design of the card cut a 1-inch (2.5 cm) slit. This slit is made along the edge of the thin white border of the back design (colored black in the picture for explanatory purposes). Fold the card in half with the back design facing outward.

1 Fold the card and hold it along the left side with the left fingers in front and the left thumb behind; the secret slit is on top facing you. Place the coin inside the folded card by dropping it in from the top—half in and half out.

2 Tap the top of the coin so it falls into the middle of the card and rests in the hole. Use the right thumb and first finger to tug on the coin to show that it cannot pass through the hole.

3 Remove the coin and pretend to squeeze it in your hand in an attempt to make it smaller. Place the coin back into the folded card, but this time allow it to go between the cards and then through the small slit. By using the left thumb to cover the half of the coin, you can display the card on all sides.

4 Simply tap the coin with the right first finger and it will appear to drop right through the hole!

TIP

This effect could easily be done with a beer mat or coaster, or perhaps even a business card. Try to make the hole only a fraction too small for the coin to pass through—this makes the effect more believable.

IMPOSSIBLE LIFT

CAST A SPELL ON YOUR VOLUNTEER AND HE WILL NOT BE ABLE TO LIFT YOU OR YOUR ASSISTANT!

REQUIREMENTS:

A strong volunteer and assistant

PERFORMANCE

 1 Stand facing the assistant; his elbows should be tucked against his sides and both arms folded up.

2 Get the volunteer to lift the assistant up off the ground by holding on to the assistant's elbows. This will be easy for the volunteer to accomplish.

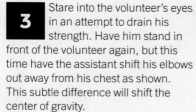

3 Stare into the volunteer's eyes in an attempt to drain his strength. Have him stand in front of the volunteer again, but this time have the assistant shift his elbows out away from his chest as shown. This subtle difference will shift the center of gravity.

4 Instruct the volunteer to lift the assistant off the ground again by holding on to the assistant's elbows. He will be unable to lift him off the ground!

OBEDIENT KETCHUP PACKET

A KETCHUP PACKET OBEYS YOUR COMMANDS BY RISING AND LOWERING INSIDE A BOTTLE OF WATER.

REQUIREMENTS:

A clear plastic bottle

Water

Condiment packet (ketchup packets work perfectly)

PREPARATION

1 Remove the label from the plastic bottle and fill the bottle with water. Leave a small gap at the top.

2 Insert the packet into the bottle and screw the lid on.

3 The left hand holds the bottle at the base between the left thumb and fingers. By applying gentle squeezing pressure the packet will be forced to float downward. By releasing pressure, the packet will float upward.

3 Experiment with the bottle and find the correct amount of pressure needed to make the packet rise and fall. With practice, it is possible to make the packet stop in the middle of the bottle.

1 Use the right hand to display the bottle to the audience. Place the bottle on the table and grip the base between the right thumb and fingers.

2 Make a magical gesture with the left hand as if hypnotizing the packet. Command the packet to float downward.

3 Instruct a volunteer to command the packet to stop. Carefully apply pressure with the right hand when he calls out, "Stop!"

4 To finish, you can unscrew the lid of the bottle and remove the packet for inspection.

TAKE IT FURTHER

What about combining this effect with another effect, such as a card revelation? You could print with a permanent marker on the bottle the words "Yes" and "No." Now you can use the bottle to communicate when finding a selected card.

BENDING NAIL

BEND A NAIL WITH THE POWER OF YOUR MIND!

REQUIREMENTS:

A few metal nails

A cloth

Strong pliers

PREPARATION

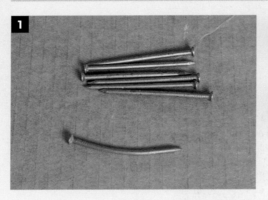

1 Place the nail in the cloth. Use the pliers to make a slight bend in the nail.

2 Place this prepared nail in the container with the other nails.

PERFORMANCE

1 Dump the nails into the palm-up left hand. Be sure to keep the left fingers curled slight upward—this will partially obscure the nails from the audience.

2 Remove one normal nail and hand it to a volunteer to examine. Explain that all nails are made out of solid metal. Retrieve the nail and dump it back into the left hand.

Bend a coin with the power of your mind!

REQUIREMENTS:
A coin, a cloth, and
2 pairs of pliers

PREPARATION:
Step 1: Place the coin inside the cloth and hold it with the pliers. Use the other pliers to bend the coin slightly.

Step 2: Place the prepared coin into the right Finger Palm position (see page 28).

PERFORMANCE:
Step 1: Borrow a coin that matches the prepared one. Hold it at your right fingertips and execute the Bobo Switch (see page 32).

Step 2: As the prepared coin lands in your left hand, make your left hand into a fist and act as though you are squeezing your fist tightly.

Step 3: Open your left fingers slowly to show the coin has bent! Casually drop your right hand to your side and ditch the concealed coin in your pocket.

3 With the right thumb and first finger remove the prepared nail by pinching it at the center of the bend with the sharp end of the nail on the right. By pinching the bend and angling it forward, as well as keeping the nail in line with the volunteer's eyes, the bend will not be noticed—the nail will appear straight.

4 Slowly roll the right first finger backward on the base of the right thumb. The left hand moves its fingers back and forth about 5 inches (12.5 cm) from the right hand in an attempt to cause the metal to bend. The right first finger slowly rolling back causes the nail to apparently bend. The illusion is very convincing!

5 Make sure to only roll the right first finger back a little—a slight bend is more convincing and believable. Drop the nail into the volunteer's hand for inspection. You can even invite the volunteer to try to bend the nail back—she will be unable to!

IF YOU CAN SEE THE MAGIC IN A FAIRYTALE, YOU CAN FACE THE FUTURE.

DANIELLE STEEL

HOLIDAY MAGIC

THERE'S NOTHING QUITE LIKE CELEBRATING A SPECIAL OCCASION WITH A LOVED ONE, FAMILY, OR FRIENDS. THE ONLY PROBLEM IS, HOW DO YOU KEEP THESE CELEBRATIONS FRESH AND EXCITING? MAGIC IS LARGELY BASED ON THE ELEMENT OF SURPRISE, AND YOU ARE ABOUT TO SURPRISE EVERYONE!

THEORY: IS THE HAND QUICKER THAN THE EYE?

It is often said that "the hand is quicker than the eye," but in reality the hand might simply be more intelligent than the eye! Our eyes often tell us things that might not be true. If your magic is convincing, people will believe what they think their eyes have shown them.

Valentine's Day will be unforgettable when you magically produce a rose from a love poem you wrote for your valentine. The next time you hear "trick or treat," you will answer with "trick" and demonstrate the presence of a ghost beneath a handkerchief!

Whether you are celebrating Independence Day or New Years, this chapter will equip you with fun and memorable magic for every occasion.

TRANSPORTING NAPKINS

**DIFFERENT COLORED NAPKINS MAGICALLY
TRANSPORT INTO DIFFERENT BAGS.**

REQUIREMENTS:

9 rolled-up napkins:
3 blue, 3 red, and 3 white

3 paper bags:
1 blue, 1 red, and 1 white

PREPARATION

1 Arrange the three bags on the table in the order red, white, and blue. The openings of the bags should face the audience. Place three matching napkin balls in front of each bag.

PERFORMANCE

1 Display all the empty bags to the audience and then turn the bags with their openings towards you. Pick up a red ball with your right hand and pretend to put it in the red bag (in reality the ball is concealed in the Finger Palm position [page 28]).

2 Pick up a white ball with the right hand and pretend to place it in the white bag. In reality, drop the red ball out of Finger Palm (page 28) into the white bag and push the white ball into Finger Palm. (This all takes place quickly while the hand is inside the bag.)

3 Pick up a blue ball and pretend to put it in the blue bag, but in reality drop the white ball and palm the blue.

4 Pretend to put a red ball into the red bag, but in reality drop the blue and keep the red palmed.

5 Pretend to put a blue ball into the blue bag, but in reality drop the red and palm the blue.

6 Pick up a white ball and pretend to put it in the white bag, but in reality palm it and drop the blue.

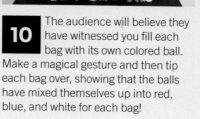

7 Pick up the last red ball, but this time really drop it in the red bag and drop the white ball as well.

10 The audience will believe they have witnessed you fill each bag with its own colored ball. Make a magical gesture and then tip each bag over, showing that the balls have mixed themselves up into red, blue, and white for each bag!

8 Drop the last white ball into the white bag.

9 Drop the last blue ball into the blue bag.

TIP

At first, the sequence might seem complicated to remember, but with practice you will be able to execute it smoothly. If you still don't feel confident, make a small card with the sequence written on it:

Red White Blue
Red Blue White
Red White Blue

TORN AND RESTORED TISSUE HEART

YOU VISUALLY TEAR AND RESTORE A TISSUE HEART IN FRONT OF YOUR SIGNIFICANT OTHER! QUICK, VISUAL, AND PERFECT FOR VALENTINE'S DAY!

PREPARATION

1 Cut two pieces of tissue paper approximately 2 by 1½ inches (5 by 4 cm).

2 Use the red permanent marker to draw a heart shape on one of the tissue papers.

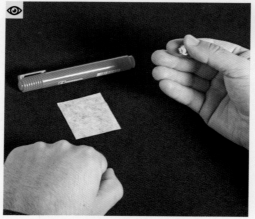

3 Crumple this prepared tissue paper into a small ball and conceal it behind the right thumb and first finger. Place the other tissue paper and red permanent marker on the table.

1 Display the tissue paper on the table. Pick up the permanent marker with the right hand (be careful not to expose the concealed prepared tissue paper under the right thumb and first finger). Draw a heart shape on the tissue paper (this heart shape should match the one you drew on the prepared tissue paper). It might feel awkward to write with the concealed prepared tissue paper between the right thumb and first finger, but it will help sell the illusion of an "empty" hand.

2 Pick up the tissue paper and hold it with both hands between the tips of the thumbs and first fingers. Tear the tissue paper in half (the tear should be vertical—tearing the heart in half).

3 Put one half on top of the other and continue tearing the tissue papers in half until they are small enough to roll into a ball.

4 Use the left hand and squish the pieces into a small ball. Hold the small ball at the tips of the right thumb and first finger. In one movement push the ball under the left thumb and first finger and allow the prepared ball to be displayed between the left thumb and first finger.

5 Make a magical gesture with the right hand and slowly begin to unfold the ball using the thumb and first fingers of both hands. The torn pieces remain concealed between the left thumb and first finger.

6 Once the tissue paper has been completed unfolded, use the left hand to hand it back to the volunteer. A broken heart has been magically restored!

APPEARING ROSE

A POEM YOU WRITE FOR YOUR VALENTINE MAGICALLY COMES TO LIFE WITH THE APPEARANCE OF A REAL-LIFE ROSE!

PREPARATION

1 Cut two rectangles out of the white cardboard, one roughly 24 by 8 inches (60 by 21 cm) and another roughly 7 by 9 inches (18 by 24 cm). Roll the smaller one into a tube and fix it with tape. Make sure the rose can fit inside this tube. It will be the secret compartment that the audience will never see. Close one end with tape.

2 Fold the large cardboard rectangle in half along its width. Keep it folded in half and roll it up. Place a rubber band around it and leave it for a couple of hours.

3 Unfold the large white tube and attach the secret compartment to it in the center along the edge of the crease as shown.

4 In a large and bold font, print a poem for your valentine on the white paper. Here is an example:

Roses are red,
They're beautiful, too,
But there's not a rose
As pretty as you.

5 Stick the poem onto the front of the large tube as shown.

6 Roll the large tube up, pour some confetti into the secret compartment, and load the rose inside, too.

PERFORMANCE

1 Display the white tube to your valentine.

2 The right thumb and fingers grip the front edge of the tube while the left hand grips the back edge of the tube.

3 The hands separate from one another and unroll the tube. From the front it appears to look like a flat piece of cardboard with a poem printed on it. The secret compartment is hidden at the back.

ROSES ARE RED,
THEY ARE BEAUTIFUL, TOO,

BUT THERE'S NOT A ROSE
AS PRETTY AS YOU.

4 Read the poem aloud to your valentine and then roll the cardboard into a tube again. Make a magical gesture.

5 Turn the tube over and quickly pull out the rose with your left hand—the confetti will fall out over the rose, giving it a dramatic appearance! Hand the rose to your valentine with a smile!

KISS CATCH

YOUR VALENTINE BLOWS A KISS AT HER
SECRETLY SELECTED CARD AND RED LIPS
MAGICALLY APPEAR ON HER CARD!

REQUIREMENTS:

A deck of cards

Card case

A duplicate force card

A small sticker of red lips

PREPARATION

1 Remove one of the lip stickers and stick it onto the duplicate force card (in this example it is the Two of Hearts).

2 Place the prepared kiss card on the bottom of the deck and the original Two of Hearts on the top of the deck. Place the deck inside the box.

PERFORMANCE

1 Remove the deck of cards from the case; secretly leave behind the prepared kiss card in the case.

2 Spread the cards face up between your hands to casually show the faces of all the cards. Execute the Slip Force (see page 28) on a female volunteer. Ask her to remember the card and return it to the deck. Give the deck a quick Overhand Shuffle (see page 18).

3 The left hand picks up the card case with the opening facing toward you. The right hand replaces the deck facedown into the case. As the deck enters the case the left hand squeezes the sides of the case; the prepared kiss card is inserted roughly into the middle of the deck.

4 Ask the volunteer to blow a kiss at the deck of cards.

5 Remove the cards from the case and spread the faces toward yourself. Instruct the volunteer to announce the name of her selected card; have her turn the kiss card around and see the kiss on it!

TAKE IT FURTHER

With slight variations to the presentation, the same effect can be themed for different occasions: A four-leaf clover could vanish and appear on a card for St. Patrick's Day, or pretend to fire a gun for Independence Day and have a bullet hole appear on the selected card!

SKEWERS THROUGH BALLOON

YOU STICK SKEWERS THROUGH A BALLOON WITHOUT THE BALLOON BURSTING!

REQUIREMENTS:

Red cardboard

A modeling balloon

2 kebab skewers

2 small flags

Tape

Scissors

Craft knife

Glue

PREPARATION

1 Cut the red cardboard into a rectangle roughly 6½ by 8 inches (17 by 20 cm). Roll the cardboard into a tube; the exact diameter will depend on the size balloon used. Print two small flags to attach to the ends of the wooden skewers with tape.

2 Use the craft knife to make two small sets of holes in the tube for the skewers to fit through. Look at the photograph to see the exact locations.

3 👁

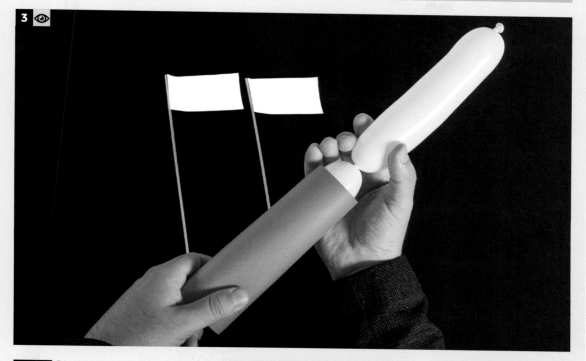

1 Display the tube, skewers, and balloon.

2 Insert the balloon into the tube and inflate it through the tube. The balloon should fit comfortably but not too tight.

3 The right fingers and thumb secretly twist the balloon. This twist is hidden inside the tube.

4 Slowly push one of the skewers through one of the holes made earlier. The twist in the balloon will provide the space for the skewer. Push it all the way through and let it penetrate the tube on the far side. Push the other skewer through the other hole in the same manner.

5 Remove the skewers and show that the balloon is unharmed.

4

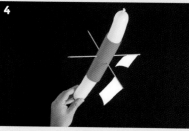

5

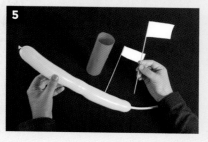

TIP

If you are struggling to get the skewers through the holes, gently pull on the balloon from each side; this will stretch the twist in the balloon and allow a larger area for the skewers to pass through. This effect is perfect for a special holiday like Independence Day.

SANTA'S PRODUCTION CONE

CONSTRUCT SANTA'S SILLY CONE AND YOU WILL BE ABLE TO MAKE OBJECTS APPEAR, DISAPPEAR, AND TRANSFORM!

REQUIREMENTS:

Red cardboard

White pom-pom

Candy necklace

Paper

White electrical tape

Pencil

Ruler

Glue

Scissors or craft knife

PREPARATION

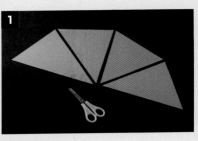

1 Draw four triangles at angles of 45 degrees on the red cardboard; the longest sides should be 10 inches (25 cm). Cut out the complete shape of all the triangles.

2 Place the fourth single triangle shape on top of the third triangle on the right. Stick it down with the electrical tape. This will form a secret compartment. Stick electrical tape along all the edges of the triangles. Do the same for the back.

TIP

If you place all three items on the Christmas Wish List into the secret compartment, you can have the audience select any item from the Wish List and you can make it appear!

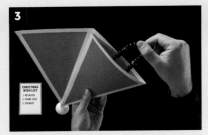

3 Fold the secret compartment closed, and then the opposite triangle flap on the left. Press all the folds down firmly and use glue to attach the white pom-pom to the tip. Place the candy necklace into the secret pocket. Make sure the sides are flat.

4 Cut the white paper into a small rectangle large enough to fit inside the cone. On the paper, print the heading "Christmas Wish List" and underneath it print a list:

1. Necklace
2. Phone Case
3. Stickers

1 Open the cone and display both sides to the audience. Fold the cone up again and pick up the wish list.

2 Read aloud the contents of the wish list. Gently squeeze the sides of the cone and the secret compartment will open a little. Drop the wish list inside the secret compartment so that it falls next to the candy necklace.

3 Make a magical gesture and dramatically pull out the long candy necklace!

4 Show both sides of the cone to the audience to finish.

A nail, pliers, cardboard, super glue, and bandage

REQUIREMENTS:
A coin, a cloth, and 2 pairs of pliers

PREPARATION:
Using pliers, bend the steel nail in half until it snaps. Cut a short strip of cardboard to go round your first finger. Super glue the two pieces of nail onto each side of the cardboard. Tightly wrap the bandage round the cardboard.

PERFORMANCE:
Slide the cardboard contraption onto your first finger—you now have the perfect gory Halloween gag!

SPOOKY MONEY

A DOLLAR BILL BEGINS TO MOVE ALL ON ITS OWN!

REQUIREMENTS:

Rubber cement

Dollar bill

PREPARATION

1 Roll the rubber cement into a short, thin cone approximately ½ in (1.3 cm) in length.

2 Conceal the rubber cement on the tip of the right finger. The right thumbs rests against the right finger, above the rubber cement. The flat top of the rubber cement should adhere to the right first finger.

PERFORMANCE

1 Borrow a dollar bill from a volunteer and display it between the hands. The rubber cement is concealed behind the right first finger and thumb.

2 The bill is now gripped between the left thumb and finger and held parallel to the floor. The right hand rests under the bill. Under the bill the right second finger curls inward and clips the rubber cement between the right first and second finger. The rubber cement is rotated 180 degrees.

3 The right first and second fingers press the rubber cement so it sticks to the center of the underside of the bill.

4 With the rubber cement stuck to the underside of the bill, the hands can be shown empty.

5 Lay the bill across the palms of both hands so the rubber cement is gripped between the edges of the palms.

6 By keeping a soft grip on the rubber cement, move one hand slightly forward and backward. The bill will begin to rotate in a spooky manner! With very little movement you can get the bill to completely rotate.

7 To finish the effect, secretly remove the rubber cement with the right hand and hand back the bill to the volunteer.

TAKE IT FURTHER:
The same effect can be achieved with a playing card, ruler, credit card, or movie ticket.

CARD IN VAMPIRE'S TEETH

A SELECTED CARD APPEARS CAUGHT BETWEEN A PAIR OF VAMPIRE TEETH!

REQUIREMENTS:

2 pairs of fake vampire teeth

Brown paper bag

Brown cardboard

Glue

String

A deck of cards

A duplicate force card

Scissors

PREPARATION

1 Cut the brown cardboard into a small rectangle with a flap on the bottom. This will fit inside the front side of the bag and will create a secret compartment.

2 Cut two lengths of string the same size and tie each one to a set of vampire teeth. Place the duplicate force card (in this example it is the Ten of Hearts) in the vampire teeth; pierce the card with the fangs so it stays in place.

4 Close the secret compartment. Place the Ten of Hearts from the deck of cards on top of the deck and put the deck into the bag. Place the regular vampire teeth on top of the deck of cards. The bag should be on the table (the prepared vampire teeth will be hidden in the secret compartment).

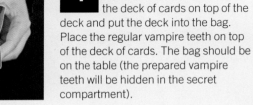

3 Place the prepared vampire teeth in the bottom of the bag in the secret compartment.

PERFORMANCE

1 Remove the deck of cards and regular vampire teeth from the bag. Briefly show the bag empty and place it on the table.

2 Execute the Slip Force (see page 28) on the volunteer. Have him display the card to the audience. Have the card returned and shuffle the deck. Introduce the regular vampire teeth and explain that you will cast a spell on them.

3 The right hand picks up the deck of cards and places them into the bag. They are quickly placed into the secret compartment.

1

3 👁

4

4

4 The left hand holds the bottom of the bag. The right hand picks up the vampire teeth and places them in the bag; immediately, the right hand shifts the secret compartment open and pulls the end of the prepared vampire teeth string halfway out of the bag.

5

5 The right fingers and thumb now pinch the bag and give it a gentle shake to mix up the cards.

6

6 The bag is replaced on the table and the right hand dramatically pulls the string up out of the bag. The audience will gasp when they see the selected card clasped in the fangs of the vampire teeth!

THE WORLD IS FULL
OF MAGIC THINGS,
PATIENTLY WAITING
FOR OUR SENSES TO
GROW SHARPER.
W. B. YEATS

CHAPTER 9

ANYTIME MAGIC

A TRUE MAGICIAN SHOULD BE ABLE TO PERFORM MAGIC AT A MOMENT'S NOTICE, WITH NOTHING MORE THAN THE OBJECTS PRESENTED BEFORE HIM.

Get ready to see the magical possibilities in everyday objects. Whether you are at a friend's house for a barbecue or making food in the kitchen, this chapter will equip you with magic you can perform with borrowed items.

Predict the outcome of a game of dominoes; make a rubber band jump between your fingers, or instantly turn water into ice! These magic effects will help you transform the ordinary into the extraordinary!

It's time to bring out the potential of everyday objects. Get ready to perform magic at any moment of any day.

THEORY: MOVEMENT TIPS

1. Face your audience: Don't turn your back on the audience.

2. Stand comfortably: Avoid shuffling or shifting weight from one leg to another.

3. Avoid fidgeting: When not in use, your hands should be relaxed at your side.

4. Be organized: Avoid awkward fumbling with your props during your performance.

5. Show clearly: Do not mask your props with your hands.

6. Move slowly so the audience can see what you are doing and follow the action.

DEVIOUS DOMINO

PREDICT THE RESULT OF ANY GAME OF DOMINOS—EVERY TIME!

REQUIREMENTS:

A domino set

Envelope

Paper

Pencil

PREPARATION

1 Print on a piece of paper, "I predict the two end numbers will be a three and a five!" Seal this in the envelope.

2 While the domino set is being emptied onto the table, secretly take the domino with the 3–5 on it. Make sure no one sees you do this—you could even conceal the domino in the Finger Palm position (see page 28).

TIP

This effect works because a complete set of dominoes makes a complete circle. By removing one domino, you are effectively "breaking" the cycle at a known point. You can easily repeat this effect by secretly removing a different domino and changing your prediction.

PERFORMANCE

1 Place the prediction envelope on the table and instruct the volunteer to arrange the dominoes in any order she likes. She must adhere to the normal rules of dominoes, that is, each number must match the number next to it.

2 Once she has completed this, draw attention to the two numbers at the end of the line. Get the volunteer to open your prediction—it is *spot* on!

DICE DIVINATION

YOUR VOLUNTEER ROLLS A PAIR OF DICE—YOU PREDICT THE OUTCOME BEFORE HE THROWS!

REQUIREMENTS:

A pair of dice

Paper

Pencil

PERFORMANCE

1 Gaze into the volunteer's eyes for a second, then pick up the piece of paper and pretend to write something down (in reality, just use the edge of your nail to make a slight noise on the paper). Fold the paper in half and set it down on the table in full view.

2 Turn your back and ask the volunteer to roll the dice and then add the numbers on view together (in this example, 2 + 4 = 6).

3 Instruct him to pick up one of the dice and to add its bottom number to his total (6 + 5 = 11).

4 Instruct him to roll the first die again and to add the number that lands face up (11 + 1 = 12). Turn back to face the volunteer and glance at the total of the numbers showing—simply add 7 to this total and you will know what number he is thinking of (1 + 4 + 7 = 12)!

5 Pick up the piece of paper and pretend to call out the number you wrote earlier (in reality, you miscall the number you have in your head); crumple up the paper and get rid of the evidence!

MATCH THROUGH METAL

A MATCH VISUALLY PENETRATES A SAFETY PIN.

REQUIREMENTS:

A match

Safety pin

Scissors

PREPARATION

1 Carefully cut the head off the match and insert the sharp end of the safety pin through the center.

2 Close the pin and hold the closed end between the left thumb and first finger. The far end of the match lies underneath the bar of the pin furthest away from you.

PERFORMANCE

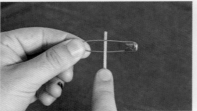

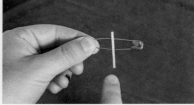

1 Display the safety pin between the left thumb and fingers. You can even get a volunteer to hold the other end of the safety pin.

3 It will appear as though the match penetrates the bar of the pin! (In reality, the match is doing a complete turn around the bar.)

2 Using your right first finger, push down hard on the end of the match closest to you, making sure you push hard and allow the right first finger to flick off the end.

TISSUE PAPER DIVINATION

CORRECTLY GUESS THE COLOR OF TISSUE PAPERS BEHIND YOUR BACK!

PREPARATION

Roll the tissue papers into small balls.

PERFORMANCE

1 Have all the different color tissue balls placed on the table in front of you. Turn your back and secretly wet the tip of your right thumb.

2 Ask a volunteer to put any one of the colored tissue balls in your hand behind your back. Once she has done this, instruct her to place the remaining tissue balls in her pocket.

3 Keep the ball behind your back and turn to face the volunteer, but secretly tear a small piece of tissue off the paper. Stick this piece of tissue to your wet right thumb.

4 Turn around, keeping the tissue ball behind your back. Bring the right hand up to your forehead as you pretend to concentrate. As soon as you can glimpse the color, you can reveal it to the volunteer.

5 You can now do the same procedure again, each time naming the correct color!

PENCIL PREDICTION

YOU LAY CARDS IN A ROW ON THE TABLE AND PREDICT THE TOTAL A VOLUNTEER WILL CHOOSE.

REQUIREMENTS:

A pencil

Piece of paper

Tape

A deck of cards

PREPARATION

YOU WILL THINK OF SEVEN!

1 Print the sentence "You will think of SEVEN!" and stick it on the side of the pencil.

2 On top of the facedown deck have the following setup: 2, 3, Ace, Ace, 2, 3, Ace, Ace, 2, 3. This setup is easy to remember by thinking of it as 23, Ace/Ace, 23, Ace/Ace, 23. The particular suits do not matter.

3 Place the piece of paper and pencil on the table. Carefully place the pencil with the prediction message facing away from the volunteer on the table next to the deck of cards.

1

1

1 Pick up the piece of paper and pencil; print in bold letters the sentence "Look on the pencil!" Make sure the audience does not see what you write; place it on the table in full view.

3

4

2 With the deck face down on the table, execute the Criss-Cross Force (see page 24).

3 Remove the top packet with the left hand and pick up the bottom packet of cards in the right hand (this will appear to be where the volunteer cut, but in reality is the original top packet). Deal 10 cards face down in a row on the table.

4 Instruct the volunteer to lay the pencil across any four cards. Once she does this, pick up the remaining cards, add them to the deck, give the deck a casual cut, and lay it on the table. (Make sure the prediction message does not face the volunteer.)

5

6

TIP

Be sure to carefully direct your volunteer when placing the pencil across the four cards; you do not want to prematurely "flash" your prediction.

5 Explain to the volunteer that she is to look at the four cards and add their values together—this will be her random secret number. A Jack counts as 11, Queen 12, King 13, and an Ace 1.

6 Recap the procedure and ask the volunteer to announce her total. Have her open the piece of paper and read aloud your prediction. She will look a little confused, but direct her attention toward the pencil—she will be shocked to find your prediction is 100 percent correct!

DICE READING

YOUR VOLUNTEER STACKS FOUR DICE AT RANDOM—YOU CAN CORRECTLY NAME THE TOTAL OF THE HIDDEN NUMBERS!

PERFORMANCE

1 Instruct the volunteer to stack the four dice one on top of the other. Turn your back before she begins so that you cannot see the dice.

2 Give the volunteer sufficient time to stack the dice and then turn back for just a second and ask her, "Have you completed the stack yet?" Immediately turn your back away again. As you say this you must get a quick glance at the number on the top of the dice stack. In this example it is a 4.

 3 Now remark that there are seven sides of the dice that cannot be seen—the one at the bottom and the six sides sandwiched between the dice. Instruct the volunteer to look at these sides and to silently add up the total and remember it.

4 Ask the volunteer if she has the total in her mind. Hold your fingers to her head and instruct her to think of the total. Wait a few moments, and then announce, "You are thinking of the number 24!"

TIP

This effect works because the top and bottom sides of a die always total 7. The total of four dice will thus be 28; all you need to do is subtract the secret number you glimpsed from 28.

WATER TO ICE CUBES

INSTANTLY TURN WATER INTO ICE CUBES!

REQUIREMENTS:

An opaque plastic cup

A white sponge

Ice cubes

A glass of water

PREPARATION

1 Cut a small section of sponge that will fit into the bottom of the plastic cup and place it into the cup. (Yellow sponge is used for explanation purposes; use white when performing the effect.)

2 Place some ice cubes on top of the sponge.

1 Hold the plastic cup in the left hand above the eye level of the audience.

2 Pick up the jug of water and openly pour some water into the plastic cup. Be careful not to pour too much water in; only pour as much as the sponge can fully absorb.

3 Place the jug back on the table and make a magical gesture over the plastic cup. Tip the cup upside down with the mouth of the cup facing away from the audience and pour the ice cubes into your open right hand.

4 Offer the ice cubes for examination and while the volunteer examines them, secretly remove the sponge from the plastic cup and leave the cup on the table.

JUMPING RUBBER BAND

A RUBBER BAND JUMPS BETWEEN YOUR FINGERS UNDER IMPOSSIBLE CONDITIONS.

PERFORMANCE

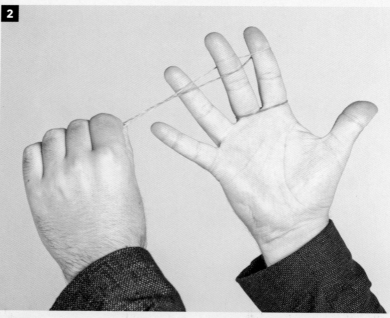

 Place one rubber band over the first two fingers of the right hand, near the base of the two fingers.

 Interlace the second rubber band over the right fingertips as shown.

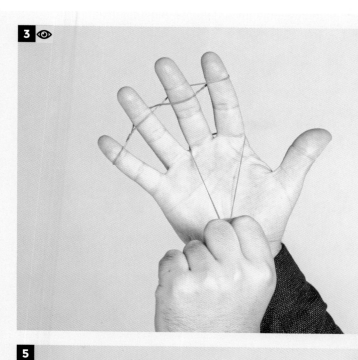

3 With your left hand, pull back on the rubber band that is over the first two fingers. Begin to close the right hand into a fist and at the same time secretly slip the top of all four right fingers into the rubber band.

4 Release the band from the left hand. It should appear as though you merely stretched the band and released it.

5 Now quickly open the right hand by straightening the fingers; the band will jump automatically from the first two fingers to around the third and fourth fingers! Quickly close your hand into a fist again.

DO AS I DO

IN THIS ANYTIME, ANYWHERE CARD EFFECT YOU DEMONSTRATE PERFECT SYNCHRONICITY.

REQUIREMENTS:

2 decks of cards

PERFORMANCE

1 Hand one of the decks to the volunteer and keep the other for yourself. Instruct the volunteer to shuffle his cards; you do the same with your deck.

2 When you have finished shuffling, secretly remember the bottom card of your deck (this will be your *key card*); in this example it is the Ten of Hearts.

3 Swap decks with the volunteer (you know the bottom card of the deck he holds). Instruct him to imitate every action you do.

4 Spread the cards between your fingers and instruct the volunteer to do the same.

5 Remove a card from your deck (but don't remember it!); place the deck face down on the table and make sure the volunteer does the same.

6 Place your card on top of your facedown deck and then cut it into the middle. Make sure the volunteer copies your actions with his deck.

7 Switch decks with the volunteer and spread the cards toward yourself as you explain that you will remove your card from his deck. Instruct him to do the same with the deck you gave him.

8 Spread the cards until you see your key card (the Ten of Hearts, in this example), take the card directly above it (if the cards were spread from left to right, it will be the card on the right). This is the volunteer's chosen card. In this example, his chosen card is the Eight of Clubs.

9 Place your card face down on the table in front of you; the volunteer should do the same. Explain that you both executed the exact same moves, and if perfect synchronicity exists, then you should have arrived at the same result—turn over the cards to show a perfect match!

CUT AND RESTORED STRING

SLICE A STRING IN TWO AND MAGICALLY RESTORE IT!

REQUIREMENTS:

Cardboard

String

Scissors

PREPARATION

1 Cut a length of string roughly 17 inches (45 cm) long and a piece of cardboard roughly 4½ by 3½ inches (12 by 9 cm) long.

2 Put a fold roughly 1 inch (2.5 cm) up from the bottom of the cardboard. Now fold the top piece down so it overlaps the bottom fold slightly.

PERFORMANCE

1 Open the cardboard with the folded flaps facing you. Place the string in the lower fold. The right thumb holds the top flap open and the left thumb holds the bottom flap open.

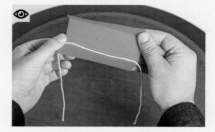

2 The right thumb pinches the center of the string and pulls it upward as the left thumb closes the bottom flap.

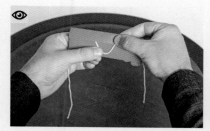

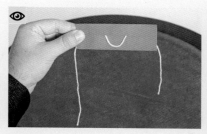

3 The right thumb now pushes the section of string over the bottom flap and under the left thumb. The right thumb immediately closes the top flap. The result is a secret loop of string.

4 Pinch the cardboard and string between the left first and second fingers with the left thumb on the back. The secret loop should stay still.

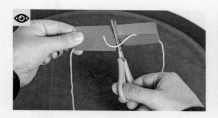

5 The right hand inserts the scissors through the loop; after the first cut the left thumb adjusts to hold the two pieces of cardboard together (be careful not to cut your fingers!).

6 Continue cutting the cardboard in two, making sure one of the halves of cardboard overlaps the other slightly—this will help sell the illusion.

7 Quickly slide the two halves of cardboard apart and reveal the string has magically restored!

MAGIC: ACE ASSEMBLY

Here is a spectacular way to find all four Aces!

PREPARATION:
Place two Aces on top of the deck and the other two Aces on the bottom of the deck.

PERFORMANCE:
Step 1: Hold the deck face down with the right fingertips below and the thumb on top.

Step 2: Rotate the right wrist to the right, squeezing the top and bottom card together as you toss the rest of the deck into the left hand. All the cards except the two Aces land in the left hand.

Step 3: Repeat the same procedure with the left hand, except toss the deck onto the table. Flip the cards over in each hand . . . the four Aces have assembled.

CHAPTER 10

MAGIC FOR THE STAGE

IT'S TIME TO TURN YOUR MICRO MIRACLES INTO MAJOR MASTERPIECES.

The stage will be your setting for your incredible illusions that involve transforming body parts into a real-life Frankenstein, sawing a volunteer in half with a rope, escaping from a sack, and successfully discovering a volunteer's signed card inside a grapefruit!

Large-scale illusions are usually expensive to construct; however, this chapter will provide you with some inexpensive but highly entertaining magic effects that will be perfect for the big stage or performance hall.

Perhaps you are putting on a show for the family or entering a talent show; your act will be spectacular because your illusions will play large with incredible props and the use of assistants!

THEORY: PROPER PREPARATION

It is a good idea to make a checklist of where all your props should be when you start your performance. Use this list every time you set up your act. You should always check that your props work and that everything is in order before every performance!

OUT OF NOWHERE

YOU SHOW TWO EMPTY CARDBOARD BOXES AND SUDDENLY PRODUCE A BEAUTIFUL ASSISTANT OUT OF THIN AIR!

REQUIREMENTS:

2 large cardboard boxes or cartons (they should be large enough to conceal a person, and one of these boxes should be slightly larger than the other)

A craft knife

A chair

PREPARATION

TAKE IT FURTHER

What about using a Frankenstein theme and have "body parts" thrown in and transform into a monster?! The boxes could be decorated to resemble a washing machine or television; you are limited only by your imagination!

1 Cut off the top and bottom of the two cardboard boxes and transform them into tubes. Cut a big square hole in the back of the large box.

2 Flatten the boxes and lean them against the chair. The large box with the hole goes in front with the hole concealed at the back. The assistant hides behind the box at the back.

1 Pick up the front box and open it up. Place it on your left with part of the box overlapping the box behind it.

2 As you handle the front box, the assistant secretly climbs into the box through the hole.

3 Pick up the remaining box and open it up to show the audience it's empty.

4 Place this box over the first.

5 Make a magical gesture and have the assistant stand up for a magical appearance!

SWORD BOX

AN IMPOSSIBLE PENETRATION! AN ASSISTANT IS PLACED INSIDE A BOX AND SKEWERED BY MULTIPLE HOMEMADE "SWORDS." NOT FOR THE FAINT OF HEART!

REQUIREMENTS:

A large cardboard box or carton (large enough for your assistant to sit inside)

25 wooden dowels

Cardboard

Paint

Scissors

TIP

To make the illusion even more deceptive you can paint a large silhouette of the assistant's body on the front of the box.

PREPARATION

1 Have the assistant sit in the box, but sideways to the audience. Insert the wooden dowels at various places and make sure that they pass around the assistant.

2 Cut out small cardboard squares and fit these onto the wooden dowels. Paint the edges of the cardboard box with a thin black border (this will help create the illusion that the box is smaller than it is).

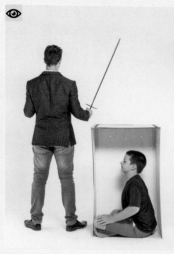

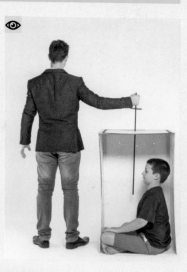

1 Display the box to the audience and have the assistant step into the box facing the audience.

2 As soon as the assistant sits down in the box, he turns sideways to the audience.

3 Begin by pushing the first wooden dowel through the center of the box from the top.

4 All of the remaining wooden dowels are pushed through the holes in the box. It appears impossible for the assistant to remain unharmed from all the wooden dowels!

5 Remove all the wooden dowels and the assistant should turn face on toward the audience before standing up. The audience will be baffled as to how the assistant remained unharmed!

ROPE THROUGH BODY

A ROPE PENETRATES A VOLUNTEER'S STOMACH WITHOUT HARMING HER!

PREPARATION

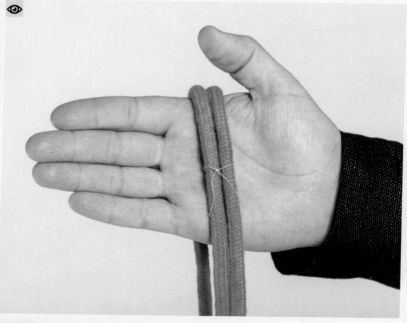

1 Use the thread to loosely tie the two lengths of rope together at their center.

1 Display the two ropes and have an assistant tug on them to prove the ropes are solid.

2 Invite another volunteer on stage. As he approaches the stage, readjust the ropes in your right hand by exchanging ends so the ropes are looped back on themselves (held together by the thread).

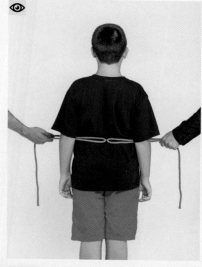

3 Position the prepared ropes behind the volunteer and hand the ends to the assistant. From the front everything appears normal, but in reality the ropes are looped back on themselves.

4 Bring one end of each rope out in front of the volunteer and tie a single overhand knot around the volunteer's chest.

5 Make a magical gesture and pull on both the ropes. The thread behind the volunteer will snap and the ropes will appear to penetrate the volunteer's chest!

THEORY: STAGE FRIGHT

Almost every magician gets excited before a performance, but there are times where you think you might forget your words or make a mistake. By rehearsing and practicing properly, you can avoid stage fright.

PRODUCTION BOX

SHOW A SMALL BOX EMPTY—AND MAGICALLY PRODUCE ANYTHING THAT WILL FIT INSIDE THE BOX!

TIP

When magically producing an item, strive to produce something that makes sense. For example, it's a hot day, an ice-cold orange juice would solve the problem perfectly!

PREPARATION

1 Construct a small box roughly 7 by 7 inches (18 by 18 cm). Cut a small square roughly 5 by 5 inches (12 by 12 cm) out of one side of the box; this will become the top of the box.

2 Cut two square panels 8 by 8 inches (20 by 20 cm); these panels will fit on the open sides of the box and act as the doors. Attach the door panels with tape in such a manner that they flip open in opposite directions.

3 Construct a second, smaller box that will be attached to the inside of one of the door panels. This smaller box should be roughly 4 by 4 inches (10 by 10 cm) and have no top. The smaller box will be hidden behind one of these door panels.

4 You can now load the smaller box with any items that will fit inside of it, such as a glass of orange juice. Hold the box with the loaded section on the back of the front panel door.

1 To open the box and show it empty, the left hand moves to the left while the right hand remains motionless. The loaded section will remain out of the audience's view.

2 Reverse this process and make a magical gesture—you can now magically produce the juice you hid in the loaded section! Take a sip.

THE GREAT ESCAPE

**YOUR HANDS ARE SECURELY TIED TOGETHER,
YET YOU ARE ABLE TO ESCAPE.**

REQUIREMENTS:

A handkerchief

Length of rope
approximately 5 feet
(1.5 m) long

PERFORMANCE

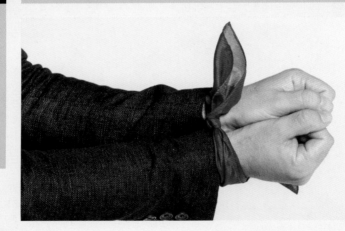

TIP

When practicing this effect,
begin by performing it with
the cover of a jacket; as
your speed increases, you
will be able to do it without
any cover as shown here.

1 Instruct a volunteer to tie your
wrists together with the
handkerchief.

2 Have him thread the rope
between your arms and
tug on it to make sure you
cannot escape.

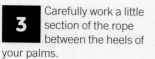

3 Carefully work a little section of the rope between the heels of your palms.

4 Continue working the rope under the handkerchief until there is a loop large enough to pass the fingers of either hand through. After passing one hand through the loop the rope is only held in place by being tucked under the handkerchief.

5 Instruct the volunteer to give one sharp tug and you will be released from the rope with the handkerchief still securely tied around your wrists!

SPOTLIGHT: HARRY HOUDINI

Arguably the most famous name in all of magic, Harry Houdini was a Hungarian-American magician and escapologist. His real name was Ehrich Weiss, and he was born in 1874 in Budapest. He performed sensational public escapes from handcuffs, straitjackets, and packing crates. He is regarded as one of the greatest showmen in the world.

MAILBAG ESCAPE

YOU ARE TIED UP SECURELY IN A SACK, BUT MANAGE TO ESCAPE AT LIGHTNING SPEED!

REQUIREMENTS:

A large sack (a gunnysack made from tightly woven burlap works best, but opaque fabric can be used)

A length of thick rope

A screen

Scissors

Eyelets

PREPARATION

1 Put the sack on the floor and hold the opening.

2 Cut several holes along the opening of the sack for the rope to pass through. Insert the eyelets into the holes to allow the rope to pass through smoothly.

3 Thread the rope through the holes and leave some slack in the rope; hide this slack inside the sack. The slack should be the size of the opening of the sack.

1

2 👁

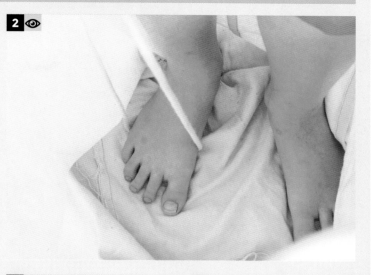

1 Lay the sack on the floor and have the assistant step into the sack.

2 He should secretly place one foot on the loop of extra slack.

3 Have a volunteer tighten the rope and tie several knots in it. The assistant inside the sack continues to keep his foot on the loop of extra slack.

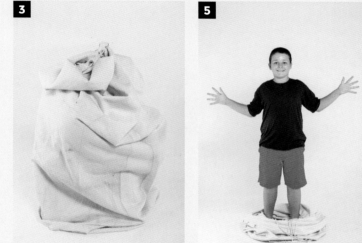

4 Place a screen in front of the sack. The assistant releases the loop of extra slack and climbs out of the sack. Once out of the sack, the assistant closes the sack by pulling on the rope and placing the extra slack back inside. The knots on the sack will remain intact.

5 The assistant steps in front of the screen to thunderous applause!

COIN IN BALL OF WOOL

A COIN VANISHES AND IS FOUND INSIDE A MATCHBOX THAT IS INSIDE A LARGE BALL OF WOOL!

REQUIREMENTS:

A large ball of wool

A coin

Matchbox

Rubber bands

Paper bag

Permanent marker

Thick cardboard

Tape

PREPARATION

1 Use the thick cardboard to construct a small tube roughly 4 ½ inches (12 cm) long and 1 ¼ inches (3 cm) wide. Secure it with tape. The tube should be big enough to allow a coin to slide through it with ease.

2 Remove some matches from the matchbox and insert the tube into the tray on one side. Place two rubber bands around the length and width of the matchbox to secure the tube in place.

3 Wrap a ball of wool around the matchbox and part of the coin tube.

4 Place this wrapped ball of wool into the paper bag with the coin tube facing upward. Place the bag on the table.

PERFORMANCE

1 Borrow a coin and have it marked with the permanent marker. Execute the French Drop (see page 30); reach into the paper bag with the coin secretly concealed in the right hand.

2 As the right hand enters the paper bag, secretly drop the coin into the tube. Use the left hand to hold the ball of wool through the paper bag. With the right hand remove the coin tube and place it on the bottom of the paper bag.

3 Display the ball of wool to the audience as the right hand squeezes it gently to aid in closing the hole left by the coin tube.

4 Ask a volunteer to unravel the ball of wool. He will eventually find the matchbox. Ask him to check if the matchbox is securely closed with the rubber bands.

5 Have the volunteer remove the rubber bands and open the matchbox to discover his marked coin!

TAKE IT FURTHER

Why only one matchbox? It is possible to do the effect with different size matchboxes by placing each matchbox inside the other; just make sure each matchbox is secured with rubber bands.

CARD IN GRAPEFRUIT

A SELECTED CARD VANISHES . . . ONLY TO APPEAR INSIDE A GRAPEFRUIT!

REQUIREMENTS:

A deck of cards

A duplicate force card

An opaque envelope

Matches

Tray

Grapefruit

Knife

Craft knife

Thin stick

Permanent glue

PREPARATION

1 Tear a corner off the duplicate force card (in this example it is the Seven of Hearts) so that it matches the image shown.

2 Use the craft knife to carefully remove the hard pip (the part that was originally attached to the tree) of the grapefruit. Do not break the pip.

3 Once removed, use the thin stick to make a narrow channel inside the grapefruit.

4 Roll the duplicate force card into a thin tube and insert it into the channel made in the grapefruit. Reattach the pip using the permanent glue.

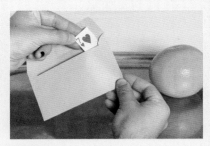

5 Hide the torn-off corner of the duplicate Seven of Hearts inside the bottom right corner of the envelope.

6 Before you place the deck of cards in the case, make sure the Seven of Hearts is on top of the deck.

1 Remove the deck of cards from the case and execute the Slip Force (see page 26) on a volunteer.

2 Instruct the volunteer to tear the card into eight equal pieces. (You might need to guide her in doing this.) While the volunteer begins tearing the card, pick up the envelope with your right fingers curled inside, concealing the duplicate torn corner.

3 Have the volunteer drop the torn pieces into the envelope. Begin to lick the flap to seal the envelope, but as an afterthought reach into the envelope and remove the concealed duplicate corner.

4 Hand this corner to the volunteer for safekeeping. Seal the envelope and use the matches to set fire to it. Be sure to reduce the entire envelope to ashes.

5 Once the ashes have cooled down, grab a small handful and drop them over the grapefruit.

6 Show your hands empty and then pick up the grapefruit. Use the knife to cut around the center of the grapefruit. Use both hands to pull the halves of the grapefruit apart, revealing the rolled card inside.

7 Have the volunteer remove the rolled card from the grapefruit. Now instruct her to see if the torn corner she kept fits the gap in the card . . . she will be shocked to find it fits perfectly!

Construct a paper tree that keeps growing.

REQUIREMENTS:
10 sheets from a magazine or newspaper, scissors, and tape

PREPARATION:
Step 1: Set the first sheet on the table and place the second sheet so it overlaps the end of the first sheet by roughly 2 inches (5 cm). Tape the two sheets together. Continue this process with all ten sheets.

Step 2: Once all the sheets are stuck together, roll them up into a tube. Put two strips of tape across the last sheet to stop the tube from unrolling.

PERFORMANCE:
Step 1: Cut flaps 4 inches (10 cm) long evenly around the tube. Gently unfold these flaps outward and downward.

Step 2: Gently put your finger inside the tube and pull out the paper tree. Give a small twist each time you pull it out more.

MOBILE MENTALIST

OVER THE PHONE A FRIEND IS ABLE TO TELL THE AUDIENCE THE NAME OF A SECRETLY SELECTED CARD!

PREPARATION

1 Make sure your secret accomplice is ready with her mobile phone on. Your accomplice does not even have to be in the same town as you!

2 Place your mobile phone in an outer pocket.

PERFORMANCE

1 Invite a volunteer on stage to help you. Remove your mobile phone and explain that you have a friend who is "psychic." The volunteer will call this friend in a moment.

2 After displaying your mobile phone to the volunteer, secretly hit the call button and allow the phone to call your accomplice. Replace the mobile phone in your outer pocket. Your accomplice connects the call and will secretly listen in on everything you say on stage.

3 Instruct the audience to remove any small personal items they might have on them, such as watches, sunglasses, keys, etc. The volunteer should collect these items and place them on the table. About ten items should be sufficient.

4 Name all of the items aloud so the audience can follow along clearly. Have the volunteer select one of the items; offer him the option of changing his mind if he wishes.

5 Once the volunteer has made his selection, hold the item up in the air and name it clearly. Your secret accomplice listening on the phone must be able to hear you clearly. The moment she hears the name of the item selected, she hangs up.

6 Remove your mobile phone from your breast pocket. Have the volunteer call your psychic friend on your phone. Instruct him to put the phone on speaker. Your psychic friend now does her best impression of a mind reader and eventually reveals the chosen item!

7 Have the volunteer hang up and return all the borrowed items to the respective audience members.

TAKE IT FURTHER

By using the same method you could have a volunteer throw a dart at a target, and your psychic friend can ascertain which number was thrown! Or do the same effect with a borrowed deck of cards.

CARD ON PADDLE

A DECK OF CARDS IS THROWN IN THE AIR. YOU CATCH THE SELECTED CARD WITH A TABLE TENNIS PADDLE.

REQUIREMENTS:

A table tennis paddle

Deck of cards

Permanent marker

Tape

PREPARATION

1 Cut a strip of tape and make a small loop roughly 2 inches (5 cm) in length. Place this loop behind a small prop on the table or simply have it stuck to your pants under your jacket.

2 Place the force card (in this example it is the Seven of Hearts) on the bottom of the deck. Place the table tennis paddle and permanent marker on the table.

PERFORMANCE

1 Remove the deck of cards and execute the Hindu Force (see page 22) on the volunteer. Hand the permanent marker to the volunteer and have her sign her name on the face of the card. The right hand holds the packet up as you turn your head away.

2 Once the volunteer has finished signing the face of the card, continue the Hindu Shuffle (see page 22), eventually shuffling off single cards until the deck is finished; this will put the force card on top of the deck. The deck remains in the left hand in the Mechanic's Grip (see page 14).

3 Pick up the paddle and show both sides of it. Place it back on the table, but make sure it is placed on top of the loop of tape. The tape will adhere to the back of the paddle.

4 Look at the audience and ask for another volunteer to raise his hand (use your free right hand to mimic the action of someone putting his hand up). Look over the audience, casually pick up the paddle, and momentarily place it on top of the deck as you use your right hand to point to a volunteer in the audience.

5 The selected card will adhere to the loop of tape on the back of the paddle. Be careful not to show this side to the audience. The moment you finish pointing at the volunteer, use your right hand to casually move the paddle off the deck. The selected card should be stuck to the back of it.

6 Have the volunteer join you on stage. Hand him the deck and instruct him to throw all the cards at you. As he throws the deck at you, hit the cards with the paddle, and at the same time turn the paddle around to expose the selected card stuck to it.

7 The cards will fall to the floor and the selected card can be shown on the paddle. The first volunteer's signature will be on the face of the card, proving that it is the same card! Carefully remove the selected card from the paddle (leaving the tape on the back) and hand it to the volunteer as a souvenir.

GLOSSARY

Angles: Some tricks can only be viewed from certain angles. A magician should always be aware of his angles and what the audience is seeing.

Apparatus: Special equipment designed to achieve a magical effect.

Close-up magic: Magic effects that are performed very close to the audience, mostly with small objects.

Deck: Another name for a pack of cards.

Effect: The trick as it appears to the audience.

Force: Creating an apparent free choice to a spectator when in reality the choice is secretly controlled by the magician.

Gimmick: A secret device that enables the effect to work, not usually seen by the audience.

Glide: A card sleight where the magician retains the bottom card of the deck and deals the next card as though it were the bottom card.

Glimpse: The magician secretly sights information without the audience's knowledge.

Illusion: Generally refers to large-scale magic effects done on a stage.

Key card: A card that is used to aid the location of a selected card.

Lapping: The action of secretly dropping an object into the lap while seated at a table.

Levitation: Making something float without any visible means of support.

Load: A secretly concealed supply of items that is later produced.

Manipulation: Generally refers to skillful sleight of hand usually performed on a stage.

Method: The secret workings of an effect.

Misdirection: The subtle art of directing the audience's attention away from what you don't want to be seen.

Palming: The act of secretly concealing an object in the hand.

Patter: The words used by the magician when performing an effect.

Production: Making an object(s) appear.

Props: The apparatus and objects used by the magician.

Routine: The order of events that make up the effect, or the series of effects for a show.

Setup: The manner in which props and gimmicks are arranged for an effect or a routine.

Sleight: A secret and skillful move made with the hands.

Stooge: A person who is secretly in on the act and aids in making the magic effect happen.

Vanish: The act of making an object disappear.

CREDITS

Many of the methods and principles shared in the book have been passed on through the years, and their exact origin is unknown. There are, however, effects that have been invented in modern times and have been published in various magical publications. It is important to credit the giants upon whose shoulders we stand. They have generously shared their thoughts and ideas and we owe them thanks.

ANIMATED STICKMAN

This effect was inspired by an effect called "Cardtoon," invented by magician Dan Harlan.

ASHES ON ARM

Prevost, 1584

THE BOBO SWITCH

J. B. Bobo, *Modern Coin Magic* (1952), 10.

CRISS-CROSS FORCE

Max Holden, 1925

INEXHAUSTIBLE MATCH

Martin Gardner, *Encyclopedia of Impromptu Magic*, Magic Inc., no. 8 (1978), 348.

KEEP THE CHANGE

Marketed in 1943 as "MIKO" by Harold Sterling. He named the trick to honor Milt Kort. Also published in *Expert Card Conjuring* by Alton Sharpe (1968), 51, as "Miko Revisited" by Roger Klause.

MAGICAL NUMBER PREDICTION

Credited to Walter Gibson (1938) and Maurice Kraitchik (1942).

OUT OF NOWHERE PRODUCTION

U. F. Grant, *Victory Carton Illusions*, circa 1955.

PENCIL PREDICTION

Inspired by Stewart James's "Hands Off," which appeared in *Tops* magazine, July 1940. Also in the collection *Stewart James: The First Fifty Years* (1989), 242–44.

RUSSIAN ROULETTE

The method used in this effect is known as the P.A.T.E.O. Force (pick any two, eliminate one) created by Roy Baker. It was first described in *Baker's Bonanza* by Hugh Miller (1968), 40.

SELF-LEVITATION

Inventor unknown, but credited to Edmund Balducci. One known description appears in the July 1974 *Pallbearers Review* 9, no. 9, p. 755.

VANISHING SUGAR

This effect was inspired by the effect called "Vanish 5000" by Brad Stine and Gregory Wilson in Paul Harris's *The Art of Astonishment* vol. 1 (1996), 285.

ACKNOWLEDGMENTS

This book could not have been possible without the help and support of so many people. In fact, what took you a couple of minutes to read took voluminous hours of preparation and research—and I could not have done it alone. First, thanks to Craig Mitchell, for his confidence in me and for entrusting me with the writing of this book. To David Gore, for his wealth of knowledge, generosity, and support with this project. David, you are responsible for making my dream a reality.

Thank you to Lance Job, for always helping me no matter what time of the night it is! Thank you to Marian Williamson and Steve Sandomierski, for sharing their thoughts and ideas with me. Thank you to Gary Wood, Tamika Doubell, and Jacques Knight, for kindly giving their time and support in the photo shoot.

And last, to my parents. Thanks for having me, supporting me, and always believing in me.

INDEX

INDEX

ABOUT THE AUTHOR

Bryan Miles is an award-winning and internationally acclaimed magician. His mind-blowing shows have taken him from London to New York. He has performed at the prestigious Magic Castle in Hollywood, California, and showcased his amazing skills to audiences the world over. He is featured on TV and radio and in magazines and newspapers regularly.

Bryan has studied the mysteries of the human mind through illusion, mentalism, magic, and hypnosis. He is a Silver Medallion graduate of the College of Magic in Cape Town and is regularly invited to teach his amazing skills to aspiring magicians. His YouTube channel, BryanMilesTV, showcases his latest clips, in which he demonstrates the incredible power of the human mind.

He is currently based in Cape Town, South Africa, and he loves to drink Dr Pepper.

Website: www.bryanmiles.com
YouTube: www.youtube.com/ bryanmilestv
Facebook: www.facebook.com/ bryanmilestv
Twitter: @whoisbryanmiles